Secrets In The Chair

A Volume of Stories

Lisa Locks

Self published by Lisa Locks (Frood) in 2024 through *We Inspire Now Books,* a business assisting authors to self-publish.

Copyright © 2024 Lisa Locks (Frood)

ISBNs
Print: 978-0-6458252-4-4
Ebook 978-0-6458252-5-1

Lisa Locks (Frood) has asserted her right under the Copyright Act 1968 to be identified as the author of this work. The information in this book is based on the author's experiences and opinions.

The author takes responsibility for their content and for any permissions to use information. Any breaches will be rectified in further editions of the book.

This work is copyrighted. Apart from any use permitted under the Copyright Act 1968, no part of this publication may be reproduced, stored in or introduced into a retrieval system, or transmitted in any form, or by any means (electronic, mechanical, photocopying, recording or otherwise) without the prior written permission of the author. Any person who commits any unauthorised act in relation to this publication may be liable to criminal prosecution and civil claims for damages. Enquiries should be made through *We Inspire Now Books*.

Cover Image: Photography by Antoinette Pellegrini

Cover Design and layout: We Inspire Now Books

We Inspire Now Books
PO BOX 133 Greensborough,
Victoria Australia 3088
www.weinspirenowbooks.com

Dedication

I lovingly dedicate this to all my clients who have sat in the chair and opened their hearts.

'Behind every hairstyle is a beautiful heart.'

Lisa Locks

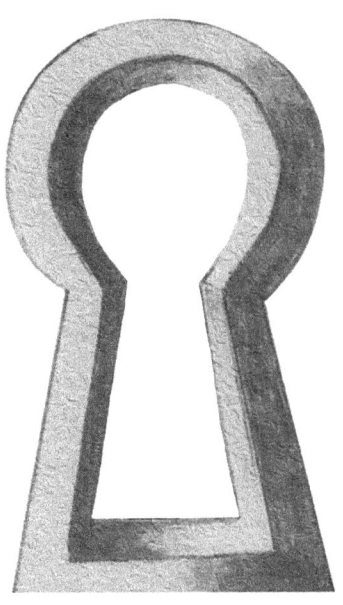

Contents

Note To The Reader		1
The Stories:		
Lisa's Story:	I Am The Key	5
Secret No. 1	Finding My Worth	19
Secret No.2:	Superman	37
Secret No. 3:	My Internal Flame	53
Secret No. 4:	Finding Love	65
Secret No. 5:	Escapades of the Anonymous	73
Secret No. 6:	Scars On The Inside	83
Secret No. 7:	My Journey So Far	99
Secret No. 8:	Finding My Voice	115
Secret No. 9:	Life Is What You Make It	125
Author Bio		137
More From Lisa Locks		141

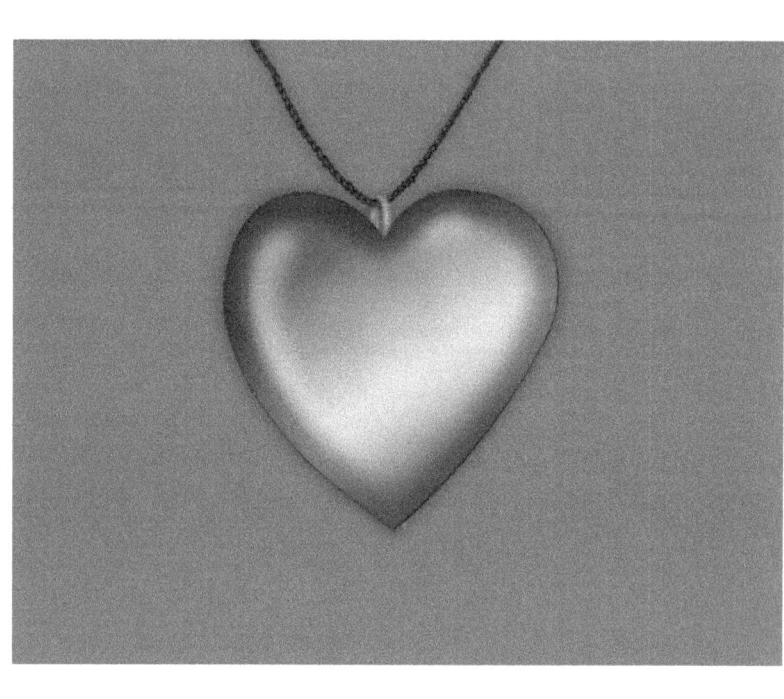

A Note To The Reader

Why I wanted to write this book?

I have been a hairdresser for over 40 years, and one of the things I have always loved about my job is getting to know my clients over the years, and enjoying the safe space to share our stories and watch each other grow. My clients often come in looking serious or stressed and leave laughing and happy. I am proud of that.

I couldn't achieve at school, but as a hairdresser, I was able to express myself and listen to my clients. I have always believed we can do more than we think we can. I am always impressed by how much people grow over the years, and how they have dealt with and moved on from difficult situations and challenges.

Their stories have inspired me, and I have learnt so much from my clients. I learn what I would like to do, and sometimes I learn what not to do. I thought others would benefit from their stories too.

I am proud of my clients and how far some of them have come on their journey, so I wanted them to share their stories. I wish to thank them for the courage to tell their stories in this book, and for revealing more about themselves.

I would also like to thank Antoinette Pellegrini and Fii Moran for their assistance in helping me make this book a reality.

Why is the book called Secrets In The Chair?

I have always told my clients, 'What is said in the chair, stays in the chair' and that it is a safe space to share. They trust that whatever is said remains in the chair. Of course, until now.

But I couldn't betray that trust, so the stories are anonymous. Each story is written by a client who wanted to share their story with others.

I am impressed by how honest and sometimes raw, the stories are, as my clients share the challenges they have faced. Their stories are emotional and inspiring, and I am so grateful that they have shared their stories.

If some of the stories raise any issues for you, I encourage you to seek professional assistance based on your personal requirements.

Sometimes, the stories I hear from clients are raunchy, and I share some of those with you in the chapter, *Escapades of The Anonymous*.

I also share my story, but it isn't anonymous. It is a story that I wrote in 2020 for an anthology called, *A Message To Your Younger Self*, created by Antoinette

Pellegrini[1]. In that book, I shared my personal journey, where I was and where I am now, and how I learnt acceptance and found the key to my heart.

I expect this book to be the first in a series, and I hope to expand the concept to video recordings shared on social media.

Finding the key to my heart is important to me. I skipped out of school in Year 10 and have been dodging bullets ever since, including depression and alcoholism. I am in a much better place now, and two years ago, I self-published my children's book, *What is the Key To My Heart?*

Unlocking Your Heart

Finding the key that unlocks your heart, who you truly are, is important to me, and in some ways, the clients who have shared their secrets in this book are finding the key that unlocks their heart.

I hope that readers will be inspired by these stories and perhaps see themselves in some of them. It's all about the journey to accept and love yourself and where you are now. I encourage readers to look within to see who they really are.

---

[1] Antoinette Pellegrini, *A Message To Your Younger Self: What Would You Say?*, We Inspire Now Books, Victoria Australia, 2020

Lisa's Story

I Am The Key

As a 10-year-old girl, I found myself daydreaming a lot, which took my mind to many places. These daydreams were often mystical, but always had meaning – meaning I was yet to understand.

One specific daydream came to me time and time again. I could see myself sitting on top of an unbelievably beautiful mountain with a gigantic, gorgeous looking tree. With me, little Lisa sat dangling her legs over the edge, looking at the world from a height so far away. From this distance, the people below looked like tiny ants scurrying around.

Everyone seemed to be in such a hurry, pushing and shoving like there was not enough time. The world down below looked as if it was passing by in a second, with the people living in such chaos. From a distance, these tiny little ants had all the worries in the world, and I thought of the saying, 'I feel like I am carrying the whole world on my shoulders.' I wondered, 'What are they thinking?' 'How do they feel?' 'What is important to them?'

Little Lisa, at the age of only 10, was already worried about everybody – everybody but herself. She had a seed in her right hand, and she chose to throw it over the edge. It landed on the ground and connected with the soil. There it was – a new tree was born. With the rain and the sun's rays, it started to grow, just like me, as the jigsaw of my life unfolds.

My Story Begins

Although growing up with a family that truly loved me, everything wasn't perfect. Mum and Dad fought most of my life; they do still to this day, and I was always brought into it. They always wanted me to resolve their fights and take sides, 'Lisa, tell us whose fault it was.' 'Did your Mum say that?' 'Who do you think is telling the truth?' I wouldn't answer because no matter what I said, I would make one of them unhappy.

After years of trying to understand and not blaming myself, I felt like I was the ham in the sandwich. At times, I didn't know if I was the child or the adult in these situations. I felt my role in the family was to make everyone get along and be happy. You see, my background was one where some in my family were alcoholics and gamblers, and others suffered depression and anxiety. At the time, this didn't make much sense to me. All I thought was that I had to keep smiling, and that would make everyone happy. Maybe then there would be peace and tranquillity.

There were times when everyone was happy. Christmas day was always the highlight of my year. I always seemed to get what I wanted, and for some reason, Mum and Dad never fought on Christmas day.

Years later, when alcohol ruled my life, I never drank on Christmas day. It was a day of joy for me. Even now, Christmas is my favourite time of year.

At the age of seven, I was diagnosed with chronic Bronchial Asthma, which I struggled with most of my life. I missed a lot of school due to being very sick, sometimes three weeks at a time. Bronchitis and asthma would attack me, leaving me breathless, exhausted, and not sleeping for days on end, having to sit up as the coughing would not stop.

I would have to be on lots of medication, such as antibiotics, preventatives, and cortisone, which would make me very agitated and anxious. So, as I got older, I needed to be on the pump to help me breathe when I had asthma. It got quite scary at times. I felt as if someone was holding a pillow over my face, and at any moment, I would stop breathing. My life felt threatened by this illness. It was very frightening as a child, not understanding the outcome of this illness, and even when the worst was over, it would take another two weeks to get over the exhaustion it caused.

This happened frequently. It was as easy as going out into the cold, being near dust, sitting on the grass or eating the wrong things – any of these could cause an attack. If I was asked to sleep at a friend's house, I would often get sick due to the environment. The simplest thing would trigger my asthma, even just getting excited or being worried about life in general. It just didn't take much for me to be sick. I was sick of being sick.

I remember at an early age, going from a Catholic primary school to a State high school; all the kids looked at me as if I had two heads. In a very short time, I was bullied, and it wasn't a nice feeling. Knowing what I know now, I can see how kids can be mean to each other, especially because of the competitiveness that seemed to exist between private and state schools.

I felt very alone and scared once again, and it was a very tough time of my life. Unfortunately, I ended up becoming a bully – and I'm not proud of that. People saw me as happy, but deep down, I was angry, and that made me a bully. I suppose I wanted to be a leader and feel important. If I could, I would take that back, but unfortunately, it was my journey.

I can only tell my story and hope others think before they choose to become a bully. It's not a nice thing to do to others. Regrets and resentment is something I had to work on myself. I even had to go to see someone about this in my later years. I had to learn to let go, forgive myself and learn the reasons why I acted this way. My personal motto is now 'being kind is always on my mind.'

By the time I was 13 and in high school, I was already dabbling in alcohol and smoking cigarettes. I thought I had found me. I loved the taste, and it loved me; well, that's what I thought. I was now wearing a mask and pretending to be someone other than me. I didn't care about what the outcome could be. I was invincible. I was larger than life. I could be whoever I wanted to be. I could say and do what I wanted.

My drinking progressed as I got older, and my asthma got worse. I just wanted to crawl up and die at times. I missed out on so much school, to the point where I was failing. Luckily, my mother would do most of my assignments, and she often let me stay home when I was either sick or didn't want to go.

I didn't understand anything the teachers were teaching me. I was so far behind that I couldn't make up the time. So, I became the class clown. There were so many incidents. Once, a boy picked me up and put me on top of the lockers. I stayed there for a few hours, waving to the students and hiding from the teachers until the same boy took me down. Another time, I was kicked out of a German class for being disruptive. I then climbed up the side of the portable and rested my head on the window sill. I was funny, and everyone laughed, even the teachers. I had already become clever enough to disguise my poor work ethic so that no one would notice.

When I look back now, I can see that being the clown made me feel very special, even loved, when I think about it. It was a nice feeling as it made me happy, but most of all, I thought nobody would notice how dumb I really was. Yes, dumb. I had labelled myself dumb!

To me, it was okay to be dumb. My brother and sister were academics. My Mum and Dad were always happy to hear that my siblings had achieved an A+ in their reports, but as long as I had a C or D, my parents were happy. I felt they had labelled me dumb too. I got to the point where I often wagged school to cope with not having to be embarrassed about not fitting in.

By year 10, I was offered a hairdressing apprenticeship, which I took without hesitation. I couldn't get out of school quickly enough. I had worked part-time from a very young age. Little me had already worked out what I could and couldn't do. 'Yes,' I thought, 'No more school, and now I can make some money!' Working for me was a good feeling. This was one of the most exciting times of my life. I was so enthusiastic and ready to learn everything as quickly as I could. I loved this job.

Now that I look back, I wish I had not labelled myself as dumb and wished I had asked for help. I just needed to be patient with myself. Being kind to others was always on my mind. I just needed to be kind and caring to myself.

My Next Journey Begins

The arguments between my mother and father didn't stop as I got older. They had both come to a decision that it would be better if they separated. This occurred a lot throughout my childhood. It had been an on-and-off relationship for all my life. I now know why I couldn't understand what being in love meant. They say monkey see, monkey do. As an adult now, I can see that I had never learnt how to love. My parents didn't know how to love each other. I had no guidance, but I do realise that they did the best they could.

It took many years and experience to find out the true meaning of love – to love someone is to love oneself first. I did move out with my fiancé at the age of 21. For me, it was an escape. I was moving out to freedom as I thought it meant that I could do what I wanted. I had my own business at such a young age, a hairdressing salon, and life was looking good. I was making lots of money, loved my job, and most of all, I could drink whenever I wanted to.

One year into my marriage, I was unsettled, confused and disconnected, so I decided to leave him. For most of my life, I was confused and upset. I felt so alone, scared, sad, worried and most of all, in fear that I would get sick with asthma. I did go back to him. He was a great man. I just wasn't ready, but I stuck with him and did my best to make things right.

By the age of 26, I had my first baby, a girl. I had my salon, a husband and now a baby. The mask was on, yet I didn't understand at all what or where my life was heading. The next two years were excellent, and I had another child, a boy. I love kids, as I can relate to them.

In some way, I felt I never grew up. I still don't think I have at times. I like to keep my childlike-minded ways. It makes me relate to my inner child and helps me to relate to other children. I love all animals too. I see parts of my personality in all animals spiritually.

Time passed quickly as my kids were growing up. I love being a mum, and I have a real bond with my two kids. My daughter is married to my beautiful son-in-law, and she has one beautiful dog. She is a hairdresser and at times worked with me in my salon, *Lisa's Locks Hairdressing*. I would have to say she is my rock, and I am hers. My son is a loving, caring, beautiful soul. He wears his heart on his sleeve and is always watching over me, making sure I am safe. He has a great job and has such good work ethics. I am so proud of them both.

My children are my world, and I do believe in my soul I have tried to show them love and kindness, to be honest with themselves, and to love and cherish every moment they have. My two kids have a unique bond that they share, and I hope they carry that through forever.

Self Discovery

But at the age of eight and ten, my children were watching me become unmanageable; my life was becoming unbearable due to my drinking. Alcohol took over my life.

Alcohol was the medicine to help me cope with my anxiety. Initially, drinking helped me to forget my anxiety, but eventually, drinking was causing anxiety. I wanted to be a good parent, but all I could think about was my next drink. Eventually, drinking became a daily habit.

Even when I was getting ready to go out, I couldn't finish my shower without coming out several times to have a drink. I was completely out of control due to the drinking. It ruled my life. I was losing my soul. I had given up, and I was surrendering, hands up in the air.

At 35 years of age, I had to be taken away to a rehabilitation centre for 30 days for my alcoholism and drug habit, away from everybody; family and friends. I didn't understand. Where, who, and why? I was lost. Was I ever going to find myself again? It was there that I found my new beginnings. I began to learn more about myself. I discovered myself.

My counsellor in rehab told me that I had the mindset of a nine-year-old child. By the time I was ready to be dismissed after 30 days, I had the mindset of a 30-year-old. That wasn't bad, I thought, considering I was actually 35 and I had grown up in such a short time. I felt I had learnt something.

I had learnt that I was going away with my own tool kit to rebuild my self-awareness and self-worth. I didn't realise then that it was going to take me another decade to catch on. The thing is, I knew right at that moment, looking back at my inner self as a child at ten years old, that I was one day going to live by example and help children believe in themselves and follow their dreams. I followed my path of wellbeing and nurturing myself, gathering over the years, as many mentors and healers as I could.

I am very grateful to have had a spiritual awakening. A spiritual teacher once said to me, 'Fake it till you make it. Take one step at a time, take a deep breath and think before you speak.' That is exactly what I believed I needed to do, to experience what was right for me.

One day at a time and I would slowly but surely grow into the person I wanted to be and make my dreams come true. I knew at that point I had to work hard at creating who I am and what I want in life, and that to me was simple. Keep it simple because I knew I was complicated at a very early age. I was different from others. I was unique, but I had a lot of wisdom to share, both then and now.

I believe I am on this journey to live and learn and to give back what knowledge I have received from the experience of my own life, but not by pointing the finger. It's through living by example. They say when you point the finger, it points straight back at you. I'm now at a stage in my life, where there is never enough to learn. I don't ever want to miss out on all the dreams I have planned, as I did when alcohol ruled my life.

At this point in time, I look back and see everything l put out there is all coming back to me. You see, about ten years ago, I made a vision board that one day I would have a hairdressing salon again, but this time in my own home. This was so I could be creative and make people happy.

I now have a hairdressing salon that I love; getting up in the morning in the environment of my own home, I welcome clients into my salon, and it is truly well worth every moment. I get to learn from so many people, and most of all my interactions are with like-minded people.

They say you attract people who are similar to you, and I'm quite happy with that. I believe we can become whatever we want to become. Once upon a time, it seems so long ago, but yet not so far away – as a child, I had created my own identity, labelled myself as dumb and believed that everybody around me thought I was dumb. I was growing into an adult with no self-worth, no self-love, helpless, unwell, and getting sicker as I got older.

Through self-discovery, I reinvented the little child from the adult form. By changing negativity into positivity, I can create the real Lisa and have the wisdom to know the difference. I am always willing to learn and discover more about health and wellbeing so that I can be an exemplary person for new generations. Therefore, I would like my freedom and belief system that I call 'my key to my toolset' to open the key to my heart so that I can love myself.

I Always Had the Key

Through knowledge, love and acceptance, I have created a key in my mind. This key has unlocked the negativity and self-doubt, which may sometimes occur. It is the simple steps that I take on a daily base. I call it the key to my toolset - in other words, the power of positive thinking and motivation. This improves my level of self-esteem as well as self-worth. The key to unlocking my self-belief and self-worth has always been within me.

My message to my inner child is to stay positive. Live with an open, warm heart. I am the master of my destiny through self-discovery and finding the courage to discover my self-trust. Through this discovery, I have experienced an abundance of self-worth that allows me to embrace self-love fully. I feel trust in myself and the world around me and thus, I experience emotional fulfilment and what I coin to be emotional success. For me, this has been life-changing.

Furthermore, my experiences of self-love and self-trust illuminate my inner awareness to trust not only myself but the greater world around me. These lessons and self-discoveries continue today.

The key to unlocking my self-belief and self-worth has always been within me, but it has taken me to look within myself to find it.

Now, at 57 years old, I am still on this never-ending journey of learning to discover myself, my dreams, the wisdom to know the difference and to bring my dreams to life. In 2020, I was proud and excited to publish my children's book, *What Is The Key To My Heart?* It took me many years and many ups and downs, but I never gave up, and my dream became a reality.

We all have a key inside us, a key that unlocks who we really are. I hope that my story inspires you to find the key to your heart.

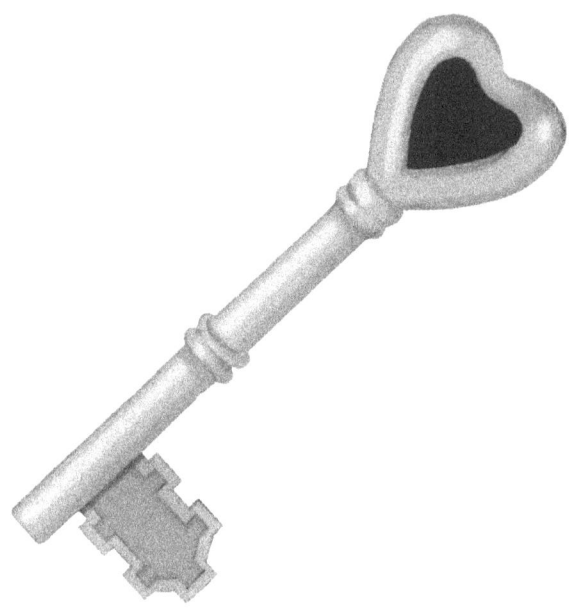

Secret No. 1

Finding My Worth

I was one of the popular girls, pretty, with long blonde hair, bright blue eyes and tanned skin. An intelligent girl, with plenty of sass and attitude. Fearless, rebellious, and outspoken. You either liked me or hated me. More guy friends than girls; I didn't stand for backstabbing and bitching. I told you how it was; I was honest and blunt. This particular night, something happened that would change who I was.

Fifteen years old, and tears were rolling down my face. It was cold, and heavily raining as I walked home that night. I felt defeated, betrayed, violated, lost, scared, and my mind was racing. How could they let this happen? Why? Why didn't anyone help? What did I do that was so wrong? Hadn't I endured enough already throughout my life?

I returned home to an empty house; my mother was overseas at the time. I showered, scrubbing every inch of my body. I hoped the boiling hot water would wash away all that had occurred that night. It was 5 am, and tears were still falling down my face. I sat on my bed. I didn't know what to do. I was so vulnerable. I phoned my best friend. He answered, and I cried harder at the

Secret No. 1: Finding My Worth

sound of his voice. He immediately asked, 'What's wrong?' I say it, the words leaving my mouth, 'I was raped, no one helped me, and they just let it happen.' My best friend said only four words,' I'm on my way.'

He snuck out and was by my side before I knew it. He kept this secret of mine. I thought it was my fault, that I was somehow to blame, that I had done something wrong for this to happen. It was my karma for all the wrongs I'd done. Like all secrets, they don't stay secrets for long. My family found out. My brothers were angry, my mother was broken that she wasn't there for me, and my father was furious. They all had my back, supporting me.

I didn't want to feel like a victim anymore. I knew that as long as I waited for this so-called man to be caught, I would always feel like a victim. The man who raped me had returned home to his wife and children. He was only in Australia to visit his parents. Things had to change. I knew only I could change this, and I did. I didn't let that horrible night consume or define me anymore. I took control. I was a teenager, not a victim.

I remained one of the popular girls throughout high school. Only now, my attitude was worse. The rape had changed me. I was more rebellious, fearless, outspoken, stubborn, what you would call 'a bitch'. I was more blunt and honest, and I had no filter. I didn't care if people got hurt by how I acted or what I said, as long as no one ever hurt me. I partied a lot, drank excessively, experimented with drugs, slept with a lot of men, some men much older than me, and I lost friendships as a result of being with some men.

I had trust issues; I trusted no one. I had a wall up, and one was getting through that wall. I made sure I was in control of what happened. I'd hurt men emotionally, so they didn't get a chance to hurt me first. Before they could get too close to me, I'd make sure I'd push them away, and cut them off; it was as easy as that. I was called a man-eater, and I wasn't fazed by it at all.

I started getting into fights and was suspended from school. I made sure people were intimidated by me; fearful of what I'd do, or how I'd react if someone dared cross me. More girls hated me than liked me, but I didn't care. I knew within myself that I would never feel so betrayed, violated and taken advantage of again by anyone. I learned to trust only myself, to be the only person I could rely on. As long as I had me, no one would ever get close enough to hurt me again.

Not long before my 18th birthday, my mother sat me down and told me we were moving in with her partner. I was furious. I had this unsettling feeling in the pit of my stomach. I knew she was making a mistake; I knew this was the wrong decision, but the move happened anyway.

The week of the move, I'd disappear after school, not wanting to help her pack, which was really selfish of me. Friday came, and my mother told me I wasn't to leave the house until I packed my bedroom. So, I did. I packed my bedroom very fast and then got ready and took off for the weekend. Partying, not coming home, and not telling my mum where I was or what I was doing.

Secret No. 1: Finding My Worth

On the Monday, I returned to what was apparently my new home. I had no classes on Monday, only spares. I was hungover, angry and had the worst attitude - angry that I didn't know where my things were. My mother's boyfriend said, 'If you hadn't gone out all weekend and helped move instead, you'd know where your things were. Your bedroom would be set up.' I didn't respond to him. I just remember the glare I gave him. The glare that said back off, I wasn't talking to you.

I showered, made some toast, and sat on the couch in the lounge room. My mother's boyfriend didn't like this; he didn't like me eating in the lounge room. I knew this, and I didn't care. From the corner of my eye, I could see the fury on his face because I was not following his rules. He couldn't keep his anger in anymore; he told me to eat in the kitchen. I ignored him. Again, he told me to get in the kitchen and eat. I ignored him again. Only the third time, he got in my face, nose almost touching mine, telling me to eat in the kitchen.

There it was. I felt that anger build up in the pit of my stomach. A man was trying to dominate me. He was in my face, and the words came out of my mouth, 'Fuck off. Get out of my face.'

Within seconds, I am being pulled from the couch, and thrown across the lounge room. My defenceless body hits the floor hard while this man is now standing over the top of me. Screaming in my face, his hands on me. I couldn't move, I screamed, 'Get off me!' My little brother ran outside to my mother, who was hanging out washing, telling her to come quickly.

My mother pulled her boyfriend off me; I got to my feet and ran to my room. I started packing my bag; I was getting out of this house. My body was covered in red marks and carpet burn.

My younger brother and sisters begged me not to leave, not to leave them there. My mother came in. I looked at her, and I screamed, 'Who does he think he is, putting his hands on me?' She tried to defuse me, calm me down, begging me not to leave, not to tell my older brothers and father what just happened. She allows me to leave once I was calm. I met up with my friends, and I got drunk.

The next morning, I woke. Mum and her boyfriend were not home. They had left for work, and my head was pounding. You know it, I didn't go to school that day, but I showered and dressed as if I had attended before they returned home.

We were sitting at the dinner table when Mum noticed the bruises all over my body. She grabbed at different limbs, worried, asking, 'Where did you get these bruises?' I looked her in the eyes, 'This is what your boyfriend did to me.' Her eyes watered as I left the kitchen and went to my room.

Not long after, my mother called me to the kitchen, her boyfriend sitting at the table. I was told to sit, as we needed to have a chat. I sat opposite him, glaring at him. He was a pig. Tears filled his eyes, and he apologised, trying to explain that what he did was wrong. I listened, not convinced by his crocodile tears. Once he'd finished, I said, 'If you ever lay your hands on me again, I will not only tell my father and brothers, I will report you to the police.'

I left the table. The next six months passed, and I had my mum's boyfriend scared. If I said, 'Jump', he would say, 'How high?' The energy in the home had changed, though. There was fear, anger and fighting, but I missed a lot of it. At every opportunity, I was out of that house. Until one night when my sister called me. Crying, hyperventilating, I couldn't understand her. The only words I could make out of that conversation was, 'You need to come home. We need you; Mum needs you.'

I rushed home, my mum and her boyfriend were fighting. I raced to a bedroom to find my younger brother and sisters crying, all cuddled up on a bed. They said, 'Go help Mum, he hurt Mum.' I see red. I was ready to hurt someone. I walked out to the lounge room to find him pinning my mother up against the wall. I jumped on his back, trying to pull him off her. He let my mum go free and yelled, 'You have 48 hours to get out of my house!'

We were now homeless. He took everything and left my mother with nothing, left us with nothing. No money, and large debts for my mother to repay; he took absolutely everything from her. We spent two weeks in a hotel, with Mum trying to figure out what she was going to do. She had no family and no one to help her. She only had herself and her children, until my dad heard what had happened. Dad invited us all into his home until my mum could get back on her feet.

All of this happened while I was in the midst of my year 12 exams. The worst timing. I saw my mum so vulnerable, hurting, and I was sorry that this had all happened. All whilst I had to try to concentrate on my exams. I felt helpless. I wanted to give her everything and fix it all. The reality was that I couldn't.

The end of year 12 neared, and I was partying hard on school nights and weekends. I was going to school, still intoxicated from the night before. I didn't care anymore; I was angry. I drank a lot, took drugs, and slept around to forget my reality. Not wanting to think about what was going on at home, I just wanted to have fun. If I wasn't at home, I didn't have to think, see, or deal with what was really going on in my life.

I finished year 12, and my behaviour got worse. I was always drinking, usually under the influence of drugs, and sleeping around. I only came home to shower, and change, and I was gone again. I was coming home in police cars and got in with a crowd that wasn't good for me. Then I met this boy, and again, my life was about to change. I was about to learn many lessons and become the woman I am today.

I was 18 he was 20. He loved to party and drink, as did I. We started seeing each other, but I hid him from my family. I know, red flag. Why was I hiding him from my family?

It was 6:30 am, and I was sneaking through the front door to find my family awake. Standing in the family room doorway, I heard one of my siblings laugh and say, 'Busted.' My mum, making a coffee with my dad,

Secret No. 1: Finding My Worth

directed me to the dining room table. I sat, and the questions began. I'd never brought someone home to meet my parents or family before, but now I had no choice. I was nervous, but when they met him, it went well, and things started to improve for me. My group of friends changed; I was enrolled at Uni to become a teacher, and I was in a relationship.

Let's fast forward two years.

'Ouch! What are you doing? Let me go.' My body was up against a concrete wall, my boyfriend's face in mine. His body pinning mine against the wall and my wrists were being held down my side. I managed to break free, and I went to run. Thud, I was on the floor. I remember looking up and seeing my best friend's face. She was mortified. She ran outside. I got to my feet, and I chased after her.

We were having a party at my boyfriend's house. I found her, and she started asking me questions. Lies and more lies were coming out of my mouth with every question she asked. Another red flag. I see that now. I lied my way out of what she just saw. Thinking I had gotten away with what had just happened. I was wrong.

My best friend was dating my brother, and she told him everything. The next day my phone rang, and it was my mum. My brother had told her all that my best friend had told him. Mum was concerned, and worried, but again, I lied. I lied my way out of it, protecting him and convincing my mum that it wasn't what my best friend thought she saw. I told Mum that if he ever hit me, I would leave; I would not stay with a man who hit me. Phew, I'd gotten away with it, and nothing like that was ever going to happen again. He was drunk, he loved me, and he didn't mean it.

His drinking got worse; it was more frequent, and he was consuming a lot more. I pulled back on my partying. I had Uni and a job to worry about. Partying was only on the weekends for me now. I started changing. I was different. I didn't know what was happening to me or what was wrong with me. Who was I? I found it difficult to go to work some days; getting up for Uni was a struggle at times. I didn't want to go out and party anymore.

Months passed, and it was my boyfriend's birthday. We all went out drinking. I wasn't feeling it, but I sucked it up and went along. Back at his house, we continued to party. I felt dizzy, my heart was beating rapidly, and my palms were sweating, and I thought I was going to vomit. I stood up, took a few steps, and I collapsed. I was out cold, not responding.

I woke in the back of an ambulance, not knowing what had just happened. I was told by a doctor that I was suffering from depression and had an anxiety disorder. I looked at him with a stupid look on my face, telling him I wasn't depressed and asked what anxiety was. They explained I had an anxiety attack, and that's what caused me to collapse. I was not convinced at all by this information.

Doctors asked me all these questions, and I became agitated. I wanted my mum. What were these doctors talking about? I wasn't depressed. I demanded I be discharged, and Mum came to collect me. They advised my mum to take me to visit my GP. I thought the doctors were nuts, and they had no idea what they were talking about. My Mum convinced me to see my doctor. I explained what happened that night, and he prescribed pills, giving me leaflets, and information about depression and anxiety. I rolled my eyes thinking they were all nuts. I disregarded it all, I wasn't depressed, and I didn't have an anxiety disorder.

Not long after that, I celebrated my 21st birthday. I had a massive party, and it was one of the best nights I had experienced. Not long after though, I felt life get hard. My boyfriend was drinking every day and large amounts of it. He became emotionally and mentally abusive. I started smoking weed when my boyfriend would, thinking it was helping; I felt relaxed, I could sleep, I was eating again, and it made me feel better, or so I thought. What was once an every-now-and-then joint became a daily occurrence. I was hooked, and life became even harder by this point.

I was in a dark place; I was not okay, but I didn't understand why or what was happening. One morning, what I was feeling became overwhelming. I cried with my Mum, telling her my life was hard, and I didn't want to be alive anymore. I was sitting in the doctor's waiting room again. I was prescribed pills and referred to see a psychologist. I was so reluctant to accept all of this; anxiety and depression. What even were they?

But I wanted to feel normal again, so I educated myself. The pills made my brain foggy, and I felt like a zombie; spaced out. I couldn't think, and I felt dumb. I wasn't dumb. I was an intelligent girl and decided the pills weren't for me. I wanted to stop them as I felt I could recover without them, and that's what I did.

A few months later.

Thud! My head bounces off a brick wall. Ouch! 'You are hurting me. What are you doing? Get off of me. Stop! Help!' My boyfriend was angry, and drunk. We had just left my best friend's 21st birthday party. I heard my little brother screaming. My mum came outside, and she jumped on my boyfriend's back, trying to pull him off of me. He finally released me, and I fell to my knees crying. My little brother wrapped his tiny body around mine, telling me, 'It's okay. You are safe now.' It was after this that I agreed to see a psychologist.

I was waiting for this woman to call my name. I was scared, nervous, and wanted to run, but not leaving that day was the best thing I did. This woman saved my life. I gained control, and strength, and I slowly started feeling like myself again.

But something still wasn't right; something was preventing me from getting over that last hurdle of being me again. What was it? Why couldn't I get there? I could feel it, and it seemed just out of arm's reach. I went from weekly visits to fortnightly visits, then monthly visits, to whenever I felt it was necessary, visits. I was feeling good, but why wasn't I feeling

Secret No. 1: Finding My Worth

great? I was sober, no drugs, no alcohol, doing really well, but why wasn't I great?

Fast forward three years.

'Will you marry me?' I froze, speechless. I couldn't talk. My brain was screaming, 'NO NO NO!' My heart was screaming, 'NO NO NO!' Two minutes, he said it took for me to respond, the longest two minutes of his life. My brain continued to scream 'No!', my heart screamed, 'No!' but 'Yes' came out of my mouth. Red flag. I should have trusted my gut instinct. My body knew I wanted to say no. So why did I say yes?

I did not love this man. The only explanation I could give myself was we had been together for six years. He had me convinced I was damaged goods. I accepted that this was my life now. Who would want me? I'm damaged goods. I didn't love him; I knew this, and we were not equals in this relationship either. He had a drinking and drug problem. He mentally, emotionally, verbally and physically abused me. He made me believe that I would never find someone else, that no one would ever want me.

I wasn't a partner to him; I was a slave. I did everything for him. He was like a needy, dependent child, and I was mentally exhausted. I wanted to leave him. I thought about how to do so often. I so badly wanted to escape; I was unhappy, and I knew I deserved better. He had me trapped; I was scared, and I was weak. So, I stayed. I put up with the drinking, and being abused mentally, emotionally, verbally and physically. All in the hope that one day, he would change and grow up.

Let's fast forward another four years.

I experienced heartache and a broken heart for the first time in my life. This was the first time I knew how it felt to love someone and have someone leave without saying goodbye. Leave without a reason, without warning. This wasn't my fiancé, it's my best friend, my dad. The first and only man I ever loved. I'd never known that a person could endure so much pain before this day. I was lost.

My dad was my strength. He was my Mr. Fix It. He was the person I told everything to. He made everything better, and I felt lost without him. Who would I turn to now for advice or just vent? Who was going to remind me of the woman I was on those rough days? You'd think a partner of 10 years would help get you through such a difficult time, wouldn't you? Not mine. Mine drank more, and his reckless behaviour was worse. He made my days harder than they already were.

Six months passed.

It was the Queen's Birthday long weekend, and I was so happy. Why? Because my fiancé had gone interstate to visit family. This meant I got to do whatever I wanted. I didn't have to report back to anyone or ask for permission. It was Saturday morning, and when I woke, I felt like a weight had been lifted from my

Secret No. 1: Finding My Worth

shoulders. I came to a realisation. I was ending my relationship; I was done.

I lay in bed and felt all this freedom flow through my body, and I embraced it. I picked up my phone and began to type that I wanted space. I wanted him to stay interstate for two weeks. I sent it to my fiancé and explained that we could talk more upon his return to Melbourne but that our relationship was finished, and that it could not be repaired.

I caught up with friends. We ate, laughed, shopped and drank. I sent a Snapchat like we all do, and an old acquaintance responded to it. This resulted in us messaging back and forth for days, then weeks. I can't explain why I opened up to him, but I did. I felt comfortable talking to him, and things started coming out like word vomit. He was someone I could speak to, just like I would with my dad. I owe him more than I think he realises. He guided me through one of the hardest transitions I've gone through - the recent loss of my father and the ending of my relationship.

I'm an all-or-nothing kind of girl. So once my fiancé returned home and I told him how things were, he didn't leave, and I became angry and upset. I just wanted him to leave, to get out of my life. For weeks, I'd avoid being in the same room as him. I would stay at work for as long as I could. My friend told me there is a process, that long term relationships just couldn't end so abruptly. I listened to him and took his advice.

He checked in with me, seeing how I was, and how things were going. I was making progress, but it just wasn't fast enough for my impatient self. My friend listened to me vent, cared how I felt, and understood how difficult it was for me in this situation. He continued to give me great advice, kept me levelheaded and checked in on me.

A few weeks passed, and my fiancé still wouldn't leave or accept that the relationship had come to an end. So, I went out for the day and saw a few friends and family. I got home late that night, and my fiancé was not impressed. I came home to him drunk, and he made accusations about me having an affair. I was nothing but faithful to this man for ten years. He wanted a fight, but I was not going to give him one. I ignored him, and he didn't like that. He did what he knew would get my attention and get a response out of me. He said something about my late father. I wasn't going to fight with him even though I was mad. Instead, I said, 'Leave, get out of my house and don't return!'

If he wasn't drunk, I don't think he would have listened; so he left. I'm sure he was expecting me to chase him as he grabbed things, proving that he was going. I didn't though, I was relieved. I was finally free after so long.

It took me a long time to have the courage to end the relationship. I truly believe my late father gave me an awakening. It was one last gift from him: courage. He didn't want his little girl to be unhappy and knew my worth more than I did. I also believe my new friend entered my life for a reason, to help me see what I deserved. He made me see sense and stopped me making excuses for my fiancé. To see that it wasn't okay, and there were no excuses for his behaviour.

My friend encouraged me to stick by my decision, and it's what I wanted, no matter how defeated I felt at times. When I was ready to give in, too exhausted to keep fighting, when I thought he was never going to leave, my friend didn't let me give up; he encouraged me to keep fighting.

Today.

I said earlier I couldn't jump over that last hurdle. It was just out of arms reach. The day my ex left, I jumped, and I felt great again. I was me. The girl who was hidden away for so long was now free. My family began to comment that they had their daughter and sister back and that I was the happiest they had ever seen me.

Life is great, and I'm genuinely happy. Things have started falling into place for me; all the things I wanted to achieve and do, I started doing. I have a great family, great friends and a great boyfriend. My friend, who I told you I owe more to than he realises, the friend who helped me through some of my hardest days, well, he became my boyfriend. Our friendship grew into a great partnership.

He is the boyfriend who appreciates me, treats me as an equal, and is affectionate, loving, caring and warm. He encourages me, believes in me, and is just as goal-driven and hard-working as I am. I've let that wall down. I've let myself put trust in someone else. I've let this man in. I now know I don't only have myself to trust and rely on. I can trust, rely and lean on him. For the first time, I know how it feels to be loved and be in love. I'm excited for my future.

I may have temporarily fallen, but I got back up, and I'm sure I am going to live my life and enjoy it. I'm not a victim. I'm not a sexual assault victim, and I'm not a domestic violence victim. I am a woman. I am a strong, intelligent, independent, caring, loving, stubborn, and opinionated woman. I have a voice, and I will use it. I will speak up, defend myself and voice how I or something makes me feel. I will never settle for anything less than I deserve, be mistreated or disrespected in a relationship. No woman or man deserves that.

We all deserve to love and be loved. I am never a second option. My promise to myself is to know my worth, be happy, love and be loved, achieve my dreams, and never settle for anything less, for I am worthy of all good things too.

Secret No. 2

Superman

I was born on 22nd December 1969. My twin and I are the youngest of five brothers, but I'm the oldest, born 20 minutes before my brother. The doctor who delivered us was well known to my parents as he had delivered my older brothers. Back in that time, ultrasounds were not available, so the doctor assumed Mum was pregnant with a large girl. I remember Mum telling us how excited she was to finally have her girl after raising three boys, so everything was prepared for a girl.

Mum knitted pink cardigans, knickerbockers, and beanies; everything was pink or girly in colour. She couldn't wait for her little girl to come into the world. Mum went in to deliver, and Dad was made to wait outside the labour ward. Expecting a large girl, it was a huge shock when the doctor told mum she had delivered a boy and there was another one on his way out. The bigger shock was for Dad. As he sat in the waiting room, the doctor poked his head out and motioned a V symbol with his fingers, meaning two kids, but Dad assumed he was signalling V for Victory, for a girl. Dad rushed in to see Mum and yelled out, 'Where's my baby girl? He looked at Mum, who was holding two boys in her arms. 'It's not a girl. We've got another two boys!'

Mum's excitement for her little girl and the doctor feeding this idea had her preparing everything in pink. So, our first year, if not more, was spent dressed in pink. Thankfully, there was still clothing from our older brothers. The excitement of expecting a girl, particularly after raising three boys, led to my mum's disappointment and possibly contributed to her postnatal depression.

Two days after our birth, we were sent to live with Dad's sister for around three months. Dad came to visit us every couple of days. Mum stayed away the whole time. We finally returned home, and life began its normality with five boys.

Life for my parents was a struggle from the start. After many months of trying to conceive without success, they adopted my oldest brother two years later. Finally, having a child they could call their own, the pressure lifted, and a year later, they became pregnant with my brother. Another came along two years later, and we followed two more years after that.

Life was quite comfortable for us but that was because Dad worked three jobs, but materialistic things were given more than love. There were no hugs when we fell over and hurt ourselves. We were told to stop crying and just get on with it. But we were as any family was, five boys messing around and being brothers.

I was 15 when we found out my eldest brother was adopted. He was around 20 when this information came to light. I had always wondered if there was something not right as he looked different to the rest of us. We were quite tall, and he was much shorter. At the time, he didn't seem too fazed by the information; it wasn't until later that he rebelled. Arguments started to surface between him and our parents, 'You're not my mother!' 'You're not my father!' and he would storm off. I was in the background observing it, but we didn't talk about it.

At age 16, I had my first girlfriend. The expectation back then was to meet a girl, get married, start a family and live happily ever after. Until I was twenty, I had many girlfriends. My joint 21st party with my twin brother was a fun night. Our friends chipped in money for a stripper. Two chairs were set up for my brother and me to sit in the middle of a circle. The striper first aroused my brother. She was naked from the waist up. She was walking and dancing around him. Everyone was cheering. She sat on his lap, facing him. She was covered in cream and rubbed her breasts all over his face. He looked like a cream pie. I was sitting there looking at him and the stripper and thinking to myself that it wasn't exciting me. This was the first moment I questioned my sexuality.

My twin brother was enjoying himself, but I was sitting there feeling a little fear as I knew it would be my turn next. All our family and friends were cheering and watching. I had to be careful of how I reacted to not create suspicion. So, when it came to my turn, I had to pretend that I liked it, but deep down, I just didn't. Looking back, I realise now I was more interested in the bouncer than the stripper herself. It had only been a month earlier that I had thought I was a little different to my brothers, but until that point I hadn't realised I was attracted to guys, until I saw this half-naked woman, and it dawned on me that she just wasn't doing it for me.

Looking back, I now understand that sex with the previous girlfriends had just been mechanical, going through the motions. I knew no different and thought that's just how it was. Listening to friends talk about their experiences had me questioning why I wasn't feeling as they were in these moments that they described as passion. I didn't feel that. My first and only full experience of a woman just wasn't for me. I got scared and didn't like it.

I was now 21. Literally, the next day after the party, I was walking in the street looking at guys and thinking just how good-looking they were. Seeing that stripper the previous night and not being attracted to her made me realise that I was attracted to the guys I was walking past, and this had me feeling very confused.

From age 21 to 27, I started seeing girls and guys. My first experience of a gay nightclub was a month after my party. My friend Luke invited me to a club, and I didn't realise it was a gay nightclub. I felt I was dressed a little too casually for going out. I was wearing jeans, a T-shirt and a flannelette shirt. He assured me it would be fine as it was more 'alternative'.

Walking in and seeing it was only men in there, I was feeling very self-conscious as I was seen as 'fresh meat'. As I stood there, back to the wall, feeling very scared, I was starting to take notice of the sexy men around me. It wasn't until the following weekend, when I returned, that I felt more comfortable and able to be myself. It was from this point that I started to live a double life.

I had a girlfriend at the time, but I was attracted to men. That second visit to the gay club led to my experiencing my first sexual encounter, and I liked it. So began the lies and deception with my girlfriend and family. I would tell my girlfriend I was going 'out with the boys'. I didn't add the bit that I was sleeping with them too. I then discovered Club 80, where men meet other men to have sexual encounters.

It was a rabbit warren of rooms, where most of the time, not a word was spoken. Simply eye contact and a nod would be enough to signify you were happy to rendezvous. You paid a $15 entry fee, and you could encounter as many men as you wanted from 9 pm to 8 am the following morning. I enjoyed every moment I was there, but as soon as I walked out, I felt so ashamed and confused. I was hiding this from my parents, my brothers, close friends, and my girlfriend. I was in this on my own.

My double life lasted from age 21 to 27 years of age. I had no one to talk to, and councillors were not known back then. Throughout this time, I had four girlfriends. I lived a lie, continuously telling my girlfriend one thing and doing something else. I would

Secret No. 2: Superman

wake up the morning after each night out and pray that this was just a phase that I would eventually grow out of, that it would eventually go away.

It was shortly after my 27th birthday that I woke up one day and said, 'I cannot keep doing this anymore! It's getting harder and harder lying to everyone! I know I'm gay!' For seven years, I had been living this double life, and I now accepted that I was gay. It was like a huge weight had lifted off my shoulders. It was a relief to admit this to myself, and I knew I had to tell my family and friends. I knew it was the hardest thing I was about to do, and I was terrified of losing all those I loved.

My twin was the first person I told. I decided that if I could tell the closest person to me, and if he rejected me, the rest wouldn't go well either. He was shocked as he had no idea that I felt like this. But to his credit, he didn't put me down and only asked if I was sure, and then he hugged me. He said he didn't care who I slept with; he just wanted me to be happy. From here, I decided to tell my other brothers, and they too were happy to accept me as I was.

Next came my parents. We arranged a family dinner at Mum and Dad's house with my brothers and their partners. We had a nice meal and later were sitting as a family watching TV and talking. I finally found the courage to tell my parents. An ad came on the TV, and my brothers motioned to me to tell them. I kept stalling for time, and they kept looking at me and nudging me to say it. Several ads came and went. Finally, I stood up and asked my parents if I could talk to them both. Mum asked if I wanted to talk to them in the formal lounge, but I said no, as everyone else knew. I could see the concern in their eyes. They had no idea and seemed confused about what I was going to say.

Saying those three words was the hardest thing I have ever done in my life. I was so scared of rejection! I had already planned what I was going to say if I did get rejected. I had practised it over and over in my head, and having my brothers and their partners there for moral support was so important because I knew that if I did get kicked out by my parents, they would walk out with me. 'Mum and Dad, I'm gay.' The room went silent. Dad was the first to speak, 'Are you sure?'

'Yes, Dad, I am.' To my surprise, Dad was understanding and accepting- Mum was the one in shock and didn't say much. From that moment, everything with my parents was fine. They accepted me for who I was, and we just got on with life.

Not long after this, I was hanging out with my friends, who were brother and sister. Their dad was a regular blood donor at the RSL and encouraged us to go along with him the next day to donate too. Thinking nothing of it, I agreed, and the next day, I found myself sitting in the South Melbourne Blood bank, answering a series of questions before I could donate.

'Have you ever injected drugs?' I answered, 'No.'

'Have you ever had same-sex intercourse?' I answered 'No' again.

Secret No. 2: Superman

My body shook as I told this lie. I didn't want to lie, but I knew if I said yes, I would be excluded and not able to give blood. I was also concerned that this would create suspicion with my friend's dad. My friends knew my secret, but their father didn't, and I wasn't ready to share this with him yet. Once the interview was over, I gave blood and then sat, had a sandwich and milkshake, and it was done. I didn't think much more about it.

Exactly two weeks later, I received a letter from the Blood Bank explaining that they were not happy with one of the results of my blood that they tested and asked if I would make an appointment to investigate further. My appointment was made for the following week.

I arrived at the Blood Bank, and the receptionist asked me to take a seat and wait for the doctor. Fifteen minutes later, a female doctor came out and called me into a very small room. There was just enough space for a desk, two chairs and a filing cabinet.

Sprawled out across the desk were various books and pamphlets about HIV. I started to tremble inside. I was in shock and devastated as I anticipated what she was about to say. 'This can't be happening to me,' I said to myself as I sat down.

'I'll get straight to the point; your HIV test came back positive. It could be a faulty test, and it could be a false positive. We need to take more blood today and investigate this further.'

I mentioned to the doctor that a couple of years earlier I was covered from head to toe in eczema and had been taking many courses of cortisone injections and cream. I was trying to find other reasons for these abnormalities that were showing up in the blood test, looking for any excuse for it not to be HIV. She said it was possible, but I could see she was brushing it off. She asked, 'Are you gay? Have you had any sexual encounters with men?' Again, I said, 'No'. I just couldn't tell her. I didn't want to be judged. I didn't want her to think that I was dirty, or a nobody.

I had the blood test and was asked to return for an appointment in two weeks for the results. That two weeks passed like two months. I was working as a painter and decorator, and as I worked, so many thoughts went through my mind. Was I going to die?

Each day passed so slowly, and as they passed, I stressed more and more. I kept thinking about the TV ads that had flooded us through the 80s and 90s - the Grim Reaper, many people laying in beds, suggesting that one person can sleep with many people and pass HIV around. Another ad showed the Grim Reaper rolling a bowling ball, knocking out people who have HIV. So much fear was spread in those campaigns, and they kept rolling around in my head. These campaigns bombarded our TV screens, and we knew no different and believed what we were told. I was terrified of what was to come.

A couple of days before my appointment, I asked my best friend to come with me for support. I'll never forget it. I had my appointment booked for 12.30 pm on the Thursday. I finished work early that day in the city, and my friend was meeting me at the Blood Bank.

I arrived at 12 pm, checked in with the receptionist and waited. My friend hadn't arrived yet. My doctor came into the reception at 12.15 pm, folder in arm, asking if I had a support person coming along for the appointment. I told her that I did, and he was running late. She said all the meeting rooms were occupied anyway, so there was time. I looked at her folder, knowing she knew the results. I was starting to panic. In my head, I was begging my friend to hurry up and arrive. So many thoughts ran through my head. He finally arrived ten minutes late.

Soon after, the doctor returned, asking us to follow her as a room was available. I stood up, and she asked me if this was my friend. I said, 'Yes'. She asked if he was coming in. I said, 'No, if I need him, I'd call him in.' She looked at me as if to say, 'You need him!' but I was in denial and continued to follow her.

We entered the room. She sat down first, and then I sat down. The door was closed. She looked at me and said, 'I'm very, very sorry. It's positive.' I stood up, turned around and punched the cabinet. My thoughts in that moment were, 'I'm dead! I'm dying. I've got no future!'

She raced out to call my friend, who rushed in and hugged me. 'Everything is gonna be ok, Mate!' 'It's not, mate!' I kept saying that over and over. But my friend was trying to be positive. 'There are treatments; you will get through this. You need to stay positive.

It's going to be Ok!' The doctor called in the councillor, who talked to me for about an hour. I was in another world. I was still in denial. I was in a blank world. The doctor didn't want me to drive home. She could see I was a mess. She was concerned I would try ending my life, which, to be honest, had crossed my mind.

But after being there for over four hours, I finally calmed down, and when they thought I was stable enough to drive home, they let me leave, knowing my friend was following behind. Just before I left, they told me they wanted me to check in to Fairfield Hospital the next morning for a couple of days so that more tests could be taken.

I drove home with my friend following behind in his car. We got home, ordered take-away, and my friend went out and brought a slab of beer. I wanted to get pissed and numb the pain, which we did. Morning came, and we woke up at around 10.30 am. I was supposed to be at the hospital, but I didn't think it was a big deal.

We eventually arrived at about 12 pm. I checked in with the receptionist. 'Where have you been? We've been trying to contact you! We were worried for your safety.' 'Oh, I'm alright! I said, brushing it off. I was still drunk and in denial of how serious things were. I was taken to a single room. Double rooms were available, but they gave me a room of my own because I was taking it so hard. When my friend left, I settled in and what was supposed to be a couple of days became three weeks.

Secret No. 2: Superman

The doctor came in the next morning. She was so beautiful and caring, like a mum. She would take her cardigan off to help you. I'm grateful for her because she helped me believe that I would be okay. She wanted to do more blood tests, which took nearly two weeks to come back with results.

Within that time, I had seen the person next door to me being wheeled past my room, with a sheet over him. I knew he had what I had. I was in shock and started to panic. Was this going to be me? Was I going to die? The nurse saw me crying in my room and came in and asked, 'What's wrong?' 'Well, I've just been told I have HIV, and the person next door to me has died of HIV! And you ask me what's wrong?' She apologised for not having closed the doors before he was taken out of his room. But that didn't help.

The next day, my parents visited. I couldn't bring myself to tell them, so I used the excuse that it was eczema and the doctors were running tests to solve the problem. During my three-week stay, many friends visited, and I told them the same story. Within those three weeks, three other patients I had gotten to know died from what I had. I kept thinking to myself, 'It is going to be a miracle if I make it through this. I'm in a lot of shit here.' At that time, I was hearing people were dying everywhere from it.

My doctor finally came to see me with the results. She explained about viral load- that I had 200,000 viral copies per ml of my blood, and I had six T cells. I asked her what a normal T cell count was, expecting her to say 10. She looked at me and said, 'A normal immune system has between 700 and 1800 T cells. They were shocked that I hadn't lost any body mass, and I looked surprisingly well. I had no defence system, and I knew things were bad.

She wanted me to have a follow-up outpatient appointment every week. This went on for the first year. She started me on anti-viral medication, and I was taking 27 tablets twice a day. They threw everything at me. I had nothing to lose. After the first 12 months, the appointments moved to every second week. That lasted another three months. There were many side effects to the medication; nausea, diarrhea, headaches, and I was so tired. I took many days off work, but I returned as soon as I could. Work helped me keep going. It gave me purpose.

It was a good month and a half before I told my brothers and their partners. My brothers were shocked but, at the same time, supportive. I decided to tell Mum and Dad. It was so much harder to tell them about me being gay. I had a death sentence hanging over my head, and it wasn't fair for me to put my parents through this, but I had to tell them. I decided to tell them on my own as it would have been so much harder with my brothers there. I reminded them about being in the hospital and told them I had lied about the eczema. I found out that I was HIV positive.

They both went into shock. They didn't speak for about five minutes. I sat looking at my feet. Dad asked if I was sure. 'Yes, Dad, I'm sure.' 'You know people die from this?' 'Yes, Dad, I know. But there are lots of new anti-viral treatments coming out.' Dad didn't say anymore. He got up from the chair and went to bed. I had no idea what was running through his head.

Mum continued to stay silent, so I decided to leave. For the next month, Dad couldn't face me. Eventually, I asked Mum why he wouldn't talk to me, and she told me that he was worried I would die. Slowly, as time moved on, he started talking to me again.

It's been 24 years since then, and much has happened. My treatment has come a long way; from 27 tablets twice a day, I am now only taking two tablets. My outpatient visits are now every six months. From having 200,000 copies of viral load per mil of blood, I now have an undetectable viral load, meaning it's dormant, but I must keep taking my medication on time every day and not miss a dose. If I miss a dose, I run the risk of becoming resistant to the medication.

In these 24 years, I also contracted Hepatitis C, which I cleared, almost lost my sight with glaucoma and had a long-running relationship with someone who tried taking me for everything, but that's for another story. What this has taught me is that I'll never give up. I am so much stronger than I ever thought I was, and I'm so appreciative of the support of my family and friends.

Things could have been so different had I not had them. As hard as it's been, I continued to have courage, and nothing will destroy me! I hold no fear, and I am happy with where I am in life. I hope my story helps others in a similar situation to not give up. I'm as strong as I'll ever be. I'm Superman!

Secrets In The Chair

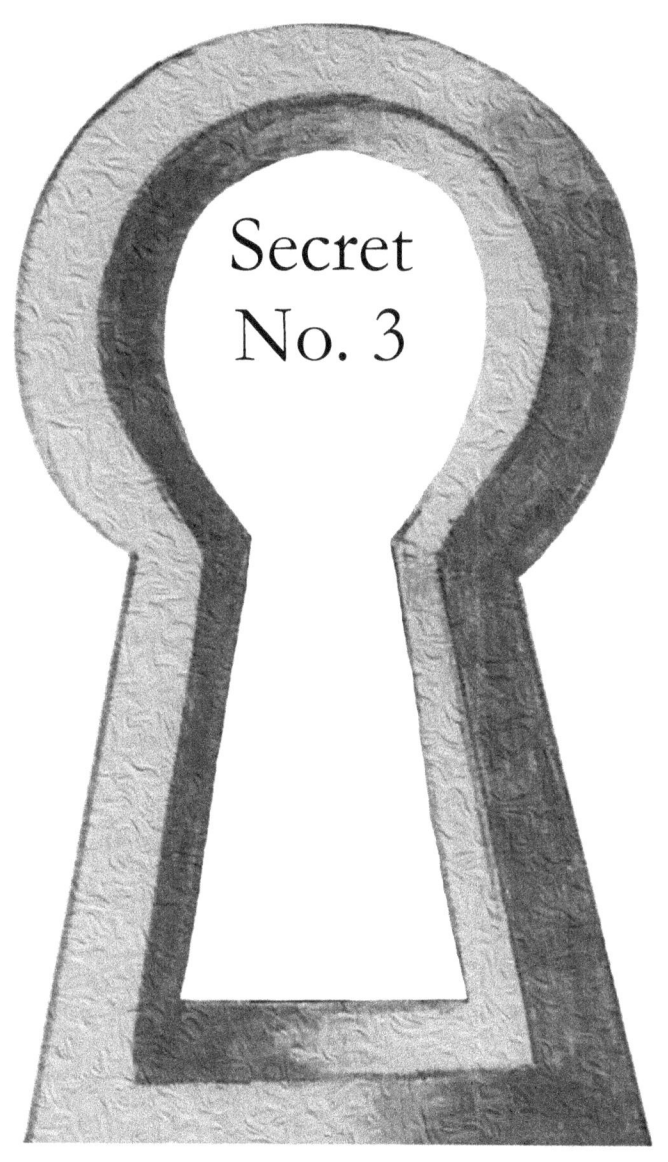

Secret No. 3

My Internal Flame

This story is about who I thought I was, who I truly am and how my self-worth has impacted my life so far. It's also a story of how, in losing my way, I've become the strongest, most empowered version of myself. Its message is more significant; it's for people to understand what damage can be done to fragile hearts from many different types of abuse. It's a *hope* that someone may read this and gain a better understanding of their own self – a better self-awareness that helps them strengthen their self-worth and not measure it against another person, validating them with empty words or taking advantage of their fragile heart.

I am the daughter of intelligent, honest, loyal, selfless parents who love me unconditionally, who taught me to be polite and show respect, and who encouraged me to think freely, speak up and always be myself. Along with my remarkable Mum and brilliant Dad, I am blessed to have had some incredible grandparents who have shaped me into the person I am today. The love and resilience instilled in me from all of them has given me the strength to get through some very lonely and sad times.

Secret No. 3: My Internal Flame

To fully understand the selfless parenting I was raised by, picture what this looked like. Neither of them was ever christened; my Dad comes from a family of Atheists, and my Mum has a Catholic family background, but no one ever attended church. They didn't go ahead and christen me because 'it was the thing to do'. Instead, they let me carve out my own path in religion/spirituality by guiding me to make good choices and forming my own beliefs. The foundation of who I am is independent, fiercely loyal and protective of anything I love or believe in.

When you are an incredibly loyal and caring person, but your confidence is low, and self-awareness hasn't developed, it can be very dangerous. The language we use about others, the way we project opinions, can be abrasive and demeaning to an individual already struggling with an internal battle for confidence and self-worth.

It'll have you measuring your self-worth based on those experiences, and it is here that it can begin to be very detrimental to your wellbeing. For self-worth should never be measured against anything but your higher self. It should be how you see and measure your own worth and never something that needs to be validated by anyone else. I have learnt this from experience.

I met him when I was looking for love in unfulfilling places, for dissatisfying reasons, with a completely disheartened outlook on myself in looking for 'love' based on a man validating my self-worth. What happened was a spiral into a dark time in my life, full of sadness, anxiety and emotional abuse.

He had been taking drugs since he was 14 and lost his father to suicide in horrific circumstances at around 20 years old. I met him when he was 27. He's now 33, and while I left after three years in the relationship, it's only in the last 12 months that I have truly come to terms with the tumultuous relationship I found myself in. If I wasn't equipped with the silence and self-preservation my family had instilled in me, my life would look very different now.

The moment I accepted he was not who I would ever want the father of my children to be, was when the journey back to my true self began. The same song would play out a few times before the time would come that I would finally leave.

Amongst the drug use (both his addiction and my own binging) was also the mental and emotional abuse and the lack of self-awareness. I'd even found him on dating apps, messaging other women – yet another nail in the relationship coffin. I had become so detached from reality and what was happening around me. I was numb from living this lie. I pushed away or was keeping anyone I thought might tap into my unhappiness at arm's length - anyone who might call out the bullshit I was tolerating or making excuses for. I was in a constant state of fight or flight.

The tipping point came when he put himself on anti-depressants, knowing after the most recent bender/fight that his standard 'sorry routine' wasn't

Secret No. 3: My Internal Flame

going to cut it. Maybe it was that, or maybe he was looking for something to take the edge off the regular Monday/Tuesday 'come down' hell we BOTH lived in week in and out. I yelled, 'A tablet isn't going to fix shit!' Was he actually for real? My skin was hot, I was anxious, and my heart was racing. I was barely balancing the illicit drug binging (his and mine); there was no way I was adding him on prescription drugs into this equation!

I'm an intelligent, free-thinking person; any occasion where I've engaged in taking illicit drugs has been a choice I made. The difference between the woman making those choices and the one now carving out her path, comes back to her self-worth. It is such a valuable and treasured part of myself that I had neglected for too long.

I remember shouting at him, 'Look at the dope you smoke every day, at the crack pipe you puff every weekend. Look at what it is doing to your brain, our life, family, friendships, and our relationship!'.

It has become hazy, but the next minute he lunged toward me, stepped up and into my face, our foreheads pressed together. He was screaming, and I could see that his body was shaking uncontrollably, his eyeballs were vibrating in the sockets. It was nothing I'd ever seen, and I had this out-of-body experience watching what was happening. At that moment, I truly hated myself, but I wasn't scared of what came next.

He screamed, 'Stop talking, stop talking!' But it was like I wanted to crack him, so it'd completely break me, 'Why! Because I'm not telling you what you want to fucking hear. I'm not putting up with your shit behaviour, I'm not ignoring your bullshit!'

With the palms of his hands, he shoved my shoulders, saying, 'Stop talking. You shouldn't be pushing me. Don't you know that I am not right!' I stepped back from the force he was applying to my shoulders. I didn't fall, but I looked down to the floor and back up at his erratic eyeballs and yelled, 'Get out of the room!' It was like he came back into his body. He backed out of the room, still staring at me, and he just knew. I pushed the door closed and collapsed mentally and physically. I crawled into bed sobbing; mission accomplished. I was broken.

There was this enormous wave of shame and grief that came over me. I could feel my Pa in the room with me that night; it was both powerful and overwhelming. He was there to keep me safe and to remind me of what unconditional love felt like, but it was muddled with feelings of being a disappointment to an angel of a man who had loved me in the most joyful way.

I was ashamed I'd accepted this as the 'love' I deserved. Who was the woman I had become? Enduring this emotional abuse and unhappiness all this time because it was all I deserved, really? I made a promise to my Pa and myself that I would find my way back and never allow this to happen to me ever again.

After so much healing, it was only when I began to understand that I was deserving of great love and learnt not to feel responsible for him, and not be hard on myself for not having all the answers, that I began to move forward.

By making his 'okay' the emotional wellbeing benchmark to everyday life, I was simultaneously diminishing the tiny flicker of self-worth inside me. Making sure his needs were met daily, carefully balancing the fuel to his erratic internal flame, and keeping it all from erupting and combusting was the day's achievement. I was tirelessly fighting the flames of a blazing, erratic, relentless addict for years.

Showing up for him, giving 100% for him, was yet another way of avoiding a moment to reflect and say you are more than this man's keeper. In comprising all my beliefs and desires, burying my emotional needs under layer upon layer of worry about him or for him, I completely abandoned my SELF.

Fanning his flames was all a distraction from the loneliness I felt from isolating this version of me. I refused to let anyone who truly knew me see this scorched soul. I felt helpless and ashamed for all the love and loyalty I'd poured into this man, hoping to ignite a passion for life, but that was still not enough. The worry and sadness had engulfed me in flames that all but burnt me out.

After months of seeing out the end of a lease in a house that had tested every part of who I was, getting myself together financially, living in separate rooms, still dealing with an addict 24/7, working full-time, still binging on illicit drugs and alcohol where I could, I finally moved out. If I'd not been so ashamed of the mess my life was and called on those who love me, I know they'd have been there and helped me out, but I felt, 'You got yourself into this. Get yourself out.'

Oh boy, I still had so far to go. I'd had enough self-preservation to finally get out, but I definitely hadn't detached from the cycle of feeling responsible, wanting to be desperately needed and loved like a little fix I needed. Looking at it now, continually coming to his rescue was a co-dependency; he was addicted to the emotional pull, and I was desperate for that 'need' to fix whatever emotional shit he had ready to sling at me.

It would take another 12 months of detoxing and detaching from the previous few years of turmoil. I was still putting a front on to those around me, lashing out at people who didn't deserve it and hurting people I loved, all while I was still fighting this internal war of heartache and shame around what I'd endured with him. In some ways, it was a form of self-harm.

I'd never move back; I'd never want to be in such a relationship again; that part was certain from the day I left. His birthday rolled around, and I called in to check if he was okay (still having those moments of sadness and grief in him losing a father to suicide). He'd been drinking and lit a fire in the backyard to sit around. I arrived, and he had literally been moments away from going up in flames. Had he not got to that tap, I would have walked in to wish him a happy birthday and found him literally burning alive. He was in a state of shock; he had burnt his legs, he was shaking, drunk and under the influence of drugs.

I operated on auto-pilot. I went to the chemist, dressed his wounds, and the blisters that had formed all over the front of his legs. I explained what he had to do to reapply, but he didn't understand the gravity of the situation, so I yet again 'showed up'. I said, 'I'll just come back in a few hours and redress it.' I wanted to shake this woman. WHAT ARE YOU DOING?

I came home and fell into this state of exhaustion. What was wrong with me? He texted something about the footy on TV, and I was in this state of disbelief about what had just happened at his house. Was it not serious? Was I over-exaggerating the gravity of the incident? He had almost gone up in flames! I texted to say that I couldn't head back that night and left it for a few days.

Eventually, he called and didn't seem as overly affected as I had been. Yet another realisation was emerging, he could have died, and I was literally physically and emotionally drained at the thought of it. Yet, here he was still doing the same shit, keeping the same habits, doing the same routine, not healing, not even trying to move forward.

Through a lot of tears, I told him I truly wanted him to look really hard at his choices, and I hoped so much that he would try to get some help and look after himself. The drug-taking, the drinking, and the unresolved heartbreak from losing a father is just a never-ending cycle, but it wasn't mine to break, fix, resolve or rescue him from.

Realising this relationship would never be enough, but not knowing what would be was the first step in accepting it was over and getting out of the blazing inferno I'd found myself in. I had to continue to be incredibly honest with myself because when I'd slip back into feeling sorry for him, worried about him and wanting to make sure he was okay, that was when the cloud of smoke set in. Smoke doesn't just make it difficult to see clearly; it burns your eyes, becomes blinding, chokes you so you cannot speak or cry for help, and it will ultimately kill you, just like flames from the fire.

I know I stepped into his world, and in hindsight, I could see he was broken from the beginning, but in my heart, I believed if I just poured more love, more care, and showed up a little more, he'd step into and up to my love and commitment, and be equal in our hearts and minds. But he lives with a broken heart and fractured soul from the loss of his Dad, and his mind is lost in a gulf of drug and alcohol abuse.

My Dad taught me never to hate anyone. 'Hatred consumes you, ' so I don't hate him. There isn't even any anger toward him. It was part of my story that I had to learn from. My hope in writing this is that it might give someone a moment to reflect on their own life and things they are experiencing, or perhaps it gives someone perspective on what a loved one may be going through. If this gives even a glimmer of hope for someone to break away, stand up for themselves, heal, move on or change their behaviour of hurting others, then I hope this finds you like I finally found myself.

In all the realisations along the way, strengthening self-worth became the vital part of evolving into the woman who now radiates love and happiness. It keeps my internal flame burning; it will rise and fall with what I fuel it or the season of my life, but when I care for it, tend to it and nurture it, she burns continuously, keeping me safe, loving and most importantly, it warms the people I surround myself with.

A woman who loves those around her unconditionally, who lives with an open heart, who finds pure pleasure in just being happy; that's the woman I am and strive to be, always and forever.

Secret No. 4

Finding Love

Another relationship ended, and I was sitting on the couch with tears streaming down my face. This time, it had lasted for fourteen months, but I was feeling more emotional and hurt than I was when my previous 13-year relationship had ended. Initially, I wasn't sure why this was the case. Why was I so emotional about this relationship? Tears weren't just flowing, they were gushing, and all I could say was, 'Why doesn't anyone love me? I just want someone to love me.'

But it wasn't me saying this; it was the little girl inside me. It felt like I was about ten years old. I felt like a little girl, not a grown woman. I was rocking backwards and forwards, hugging myself. I was hurting and just wanted someone to love me, but at the same time, feeling that maybe I wasn't worthy of love. I felt such a yearning, 'Why doesn't anyone love me? I just want someone to love me.'

This wasn't just about the end of my current relationship. This was much deeper. Something from the core of who I was. This was my inner self, my

Secret No.4: Finding Love

inner child, crying, yearning for a love I never had. The tears streaming down my face were tears from years of hurt, fifty years of yearning for love and acceptance, starting from the love I wanted from my parents.

I now know that Mum and Dad did love me, but they didn't know how to show it in the way I needed. They fed, clothed, educated, and cared for my physical needs, but I wanted a hug and to be told that they loved me, and that I was lovable, but that never happened. This is not entirely true. A few years before she died, my mother did tell me she loved me and hugged me, but it was when I was a little girl that I needed it. I didn't get love and hugs back then when I needed it most.

Perhaps they didn't know how. Perhaps They didn't feel loved themselves.

Even from a young age, I knew my parents didn't love each other much. That was obvious. I saw the difference between them and other couples I knew, even people we were related to and who were of similar age to Mum and Dad. There was little affection between them, yet they stayed together. I know that Mum was angry and upset most of the time because, quite often, she would explode over something that my siblings and I had done.

It was never anything serious. Perhaps we were squabbling with each other or playing too loudly, but every so often, Mum would 'lose it'. She would start screaming, and then any plate, cup, or glass within her reach would end up smashed on the floor. This would last for minutes, but it seemed like forever. We would then have to clean it up.

These outbursts terrified us, and of course, we took it personally and thought we must really be bad, but even then, I also felt a sense of injustice. I knew that this was an overreaction. Surely, what we had done didn't warrant this outburst. When I was older, I started to realise that she must have been bottling up hurt and anger against Dad, and we wore the brunt of it.

Yet, Dad would occasionally try to show affection to Mum, especially at parties, when he had a little more to drink than usual. Still, she was never very accepting of his advances, and generally, there was little love between them. So how could they show love to me? Of course, I didn't understand this when I was young.

A few years after my dad passed at the age of 79, my mother shared a secret with me. A secret she had kept all her life and had never told anyone. She was talking to me about dad, as she often did, repeating the stories she had told me many times before about how he had treated her when she suddenly stopped and said, 'You know your dad raped me before we were married.'

I was shocked. What? What do you mean? What happened? Then she told me her story.

She said that Dad had passionately pursued her and wanted to marry her. As it was in those days in Italy, they never met alone. He would walk with her in the

Secret No.4: Finding Love

street, chaperoned of course, or visit her house. Mum wasn't keen when Dad asked her father for her hand in marriage, but her family and friends convinced her it was a good match. Dad came from a wealthier family, and Mum's family was relatively poor, so that was a significant factor in Mum's compliant response. As she explained to me, she reluctantly agreed. Arranged and semi-arranged marriages were the norm back then.

But late at night, three days before their wedding, Dad managed to sneak into Mum's house. Her house consisted of five rooms, one on top of each other, with the kitchen on the ground level. Dad managed to get in and hide in the pantry cupboard, waiting for Mum to come into the kitchen to get a drink.

How did he know she would do that? Mum wasn't sure, but she did go down to get a drink that night, and Dad took the opportunity to grab her and push her into the cupboard. At first, he just kissed her, but then it went further. Mum told him to stop, but he didn't.

Mum was devastated, distraught and violated. She thought, 'How could he do this to me?'

Being a virgin on her wedding day meant a great deal to Mum. Culturally, it was all-important. This was not what she wanted for her first sexual encounter with Dad. She now felt she had no choice but to marry him. She was no longer a virgin, so she couldn't marry anyone else.

I don't know what Dad's motivation was, but I think Mum lost respect for Dad from that time.

When she stopped talking, I didn't know what to say. Should I hate my dad? I couldn't hate him, but I now understood why Mum found it difficult to show him any real love. Yet, I also know that Dad wanted Mum to love him. He wanted to be loved. No wonder they couldn't show me love; they probably didn't love themselves and certainly struggled to love each other.

So, it's no surprise that I found myself crying at the end of another relationship. Now, I understand why. I entered relationships too quickly, ones that I shouldn't have entered, ones I knew weren't right for me because I craved love. They said they wanted me; they loved me, so I ignored the red flags. Sometimes, the flags were the size of the large football banners teams run through on Grand Final day, but I still ignored them. I just wanted someone to love me.

The problem was that I didn't feel worthy of love, so I accepted things that I shouldn't have accepted, didn't argue so I wouldn't rock the boat, and I lost myself in the process. I remember looking around my house at the end of my first marriage and thinking that there was nothing in my house that represented me, that I had chosen, or that I even liked. Where had I gone?

Just before my mother passed at the age of 90, she told me that she had never been with any man except for my father. She saw that as a badge of honour and felt that it was important I know that. I thought how sad it was that she had never experienced real love.

Secret No.4: Finding Love

Have I experienced love? To some extent, I have. I loved the men I was with, and most have loved me in return, but it has never felt like the unconditional love that comes from the total acceptance of another person.

I know this is because I didn't love myself enough. I accepted less than I should. If you don't fully accept yourself, then how can anyone else accept you?

Perhaps my marriages and relationships were all doomed to end from the start. I accepted less than I deserved; I wasn't truly myself. I didn't rock the boat or stand up for myself or what was important to me. I remember thinking many times, 'If I push this point, it might end the relationship,' and each time, I backed down.

I shouldn't have done that. I should have talked it through and told my partner what was important to me. It might have ended some of the relationships, but who knows, if they didn't end, then they may have been much better as they would have been on a more authentic footing.

So now I find myself at age 60, without a relationship that I have always craved, but this time, I am not rushing back to find a man who says they will love me. This time, I will take the time to love myself and discover more of who I am and what I want in a relationship.

I have finally understood that the best relationship is the one you have with yourself - that the best love you will have is the love you have for yourself. Once I value and love myself, I will then attract the man who values and loves me, and even if that doesn't happen, I will still feel loved because the love will be within me.

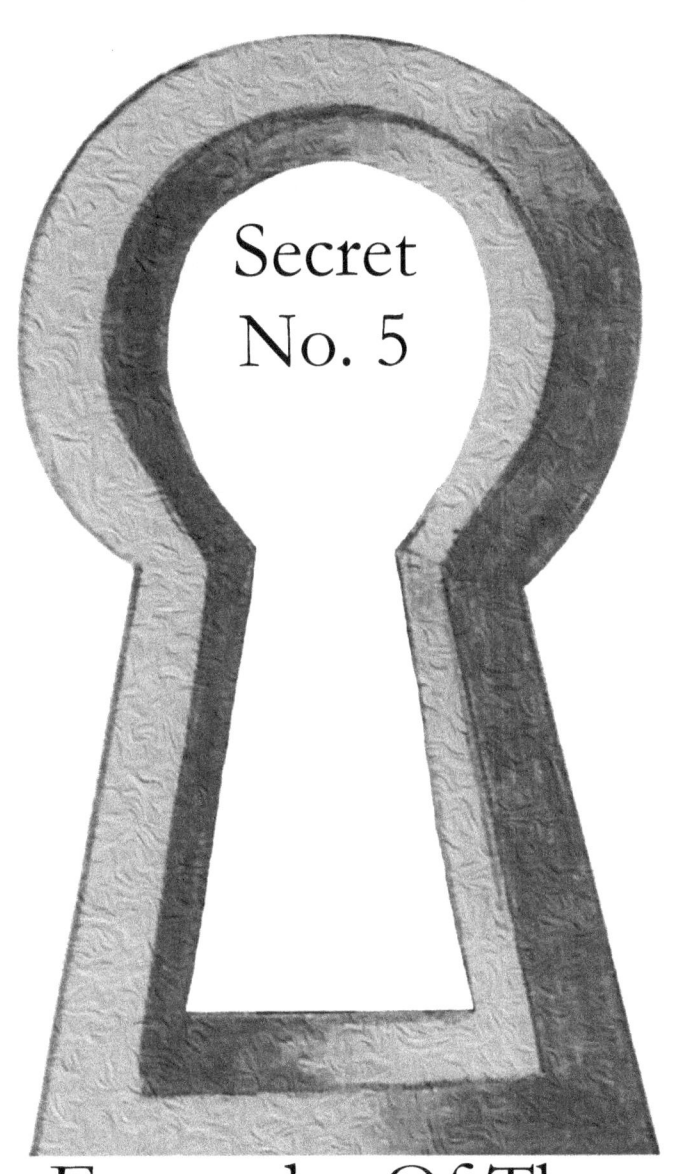

Secret No. 5

Escapades Of The Anonymous

The unsealed sealed section.
A collection of short, sometimes raunchy tales.

Concierge Man

The Facebook messages kept popping up, just like his member, right there in my face. No shame on his part with the repeated, 'I'm your long-lost friend nudie pics'. For me, the expletives came easy. 'What the…!' I scrolled on, as you do when one is neither attracted or turned on by a full-frontal photo.

Life went on.

Sometime later, whilst doing a course, a friend and I ended up lost trying to find where we'd parked our car. You know, those really silly situations where you just forget, lol. We found a door, went through it, thinking it was the right way and ended up in a laneway! Where the bloody hell are we?

With no idea, we headed for the main street. As we rush around the corner, BANG!! I bumped full-on into a man standing out front of the hotel we had now found ourselves in front of. I am not sure whether the guy realised, but I definitely did. It seems the guy who is the Concierge Man to everyone else, is Mr FB nudie pic man to me. A quick getaway to find the car was in order.

The Locksmith

Even 40-somethings can still have a bit of fun! The girl's night was happening, and here we were, a full carload heading out for the night. What a fabulous idea to issue a challenge; who would pick up first? Haha. Never one to back down from a challenge, I quietly accepted and then saw it. Driving next to our car was a white van with signwriting: LOCKSMITH and a pretty good-looking dark-haired guy driving. This was my chance to win, and our night hadn't even really started! Go Me.

Sitting in the backseat of the car, I discreetly dialled the phone number that was clearly displayed on the van. He answered. I told him I was sitting in the back seat and waved. He must've thought I was a bit of alright, and that was it, date made! Hey girls, I win! Haha

Date night came, and I was ready for a night of passion with the tall, dark-haired locksmith. Well, turns out my night of passion was listening to a separated man's tale of woe. Getting it on with a sad, tattooed biker in a dingy motel definitely wasn't my plan. At that moment, I realised I needed to be my own locksmith and get the hell outta there.

Dangerous Liaison

The dating app supplied me with a good-looking European man, not my usual type, but hey, I was out for a good time. He picked me up to go out for dinner, you know, wine and dine, hehe. He drove a snazzy sportscar, which I thought was cool. He had the music blaring and was doing dance moves especially round corners. At first, I thought, oh yeah, that's funny, then realised there was a clunkity clunk noise with his exaggerated moves as we turned corners. Strange that.

We arrived at the restaurant and had a nice meal and a drink before heading to his place. I'd had a few drinks at home, so one with dinner, I guess, was okay. On the drive to his apartment, he turned the music up again to perform his dance moves, or were they his dating mating moves? Haha, who knows? But the clunkity clunk was still there.

I wanted to ask what the heck the noise was, but the little voice inside me decided it wasn't the right time; stick to playing the role of the dating girl. So, I did and made it home the next day, never to see him again.

Until, a few years later, a friend told me to turn on the news. There he was, Mr Mysterious was up for murder. I can now only imagine what the clunkity clunk noise in his car was.

The Sexy Stranger

As a newly single 40-something, I gladly accepted the invitation to the birthday party. It'd be a bit of fun with friends, which was well overdue. I had been busy with work and fitness training, so I was in great shape and wanted to let my hair down a little. It was a balmy summer evening, great for a pool party and BBQ. The night was going great. Everyone was having fun, enjoying food and drinks, and there was lots of laughter.

I was chatting with a girlfriend when a young, well-built guy introduced himself to me. We started chatting, and I was flattered a younger man was interested in little old me. After a few minutes, a rather elegantly tall, well over 6 foot tall, guy bounds over and interrupts the conversation to introduce himself.

Well, here I am thinking to myself, what the hell, not one but two young dudes. I didn't consider myself a cougar, but perhaps I should, haha.

Turns out they were brothers, and the very tall one is older, so he sent his younger brother on his merry way. A little bit of sibling rivalry ensues, and the first guy heads off to chat with other people. Somehow, the elegant giant had my heart a flutter, and it was nice to receive some male attention.

The night was coming to a close, and people were saying their goodbyes in dribs and drabs. Heading up the drive, I spied Mr Tall and went to say bye. He swept me up into his arms, lifting me off the ground just like an elegant dance move, passionately kissing me. Woah, that was unexpected, so was his brother's voice I heard behind us say, ' I saw her first.' There it was, my first cougar encounter with a sexy stranger.

BasementBanker

The office in the bank was busy. The hustle and bustle of customers, phones ringing, computers dinging. Old staff were leaving, and new staff were coming on board. Then there he was, the new supervisor. He was tall, handsome, had a neat moustache and was wearing a suit and tie. Our eyes met, a mutual smile, and we ended up getting along great. So great, in fact, we'd call each other from the same side of the office just to chat to alleviate other people's suspicions there was 'something going on'.

Old records were filed in the basement. It was dark, dusty and a little spooky, being an old bluestone CBD building. Not one to shirk responsibility, I offered to give the handsome supervisor a tour whilst taking the filing downstairs. Off we headed, down the cold stone stairway, past the locked safe, staff toilets round the corner to the big heavy basement records room doors.

The air was cold, yet I felt hot. He stood next to me, and as I was talking, explaining the layout of the records room, he reached for me, and I went silent, sinking into his strong arms as we disappeared from the world for a moment. It wasn't what I'd banked on, but hey, it was a fine transaction.

The Lift

The old bank had a lift used by staff over three levels. The fun we had in those brief moments was priceless. We could let our hair down without the questioning judging eyes of customers, laugh our sillies out and be a bit raucous, then back to being serious bankers.

On one ride, it was just me and a loans officer. I had noticed him checking me out a few times; I just smiled and thought nothing of it. Until we were alone together, the lift doors closed and we started going up. Then bang, the lift halted. He'd pressed the stop button. For a few seconds, the cold cube became a hot box with two bodies entwined in a stolen kiss.

If only the lift could talk, I wonder what secrets it would have to share?!

CB Mac

Saturday nights were boring until I discovered how much fun it was to chat with random people over the radio waves. (I had attended an all-girls school and had an overprotective father, and strict mother, so it was refreshing and exciting, to talk with males!) Yep, back in the days before mobile phones, the humble CB radio was cool, lol. I convinced Mum it was harmless fun and to let me hang out in her car after church on Saturday nights.

So, there I was by the dashboard light of her HR Holden sedan, parked safely under the carport behind the roller door. I turned on the CB radio, set the squelch and volume dials just right, picked up the handset and was ready to rock and roll.

Breaker, breaker, anyone online?

I waited. There was the usual static and a few voices, then one I had not heard before.

10-4 This is Mac, what's your handle?

Hey Mac, YL here. What are you up to?

The conversation continued. We talked about everyday young person stuff, sometimes a little cheekier than others. We swapped our 20's (we lived quite close), got to know each other and made CB dates each week. Perhaps it was his smooth deep voice that made me melt like butter; I wanted to meet this guy named Mac. So, I plucked up the courage, and we arranged an eyeball.

Secret No. 5: Escapades Of The Anonymous

The night arrived. Eyeball time. I was a bit too excited, maybe, but hey, life's meant to be fun, right?! I hoped Mac was as hot in person as he sounded! I didn't have my licence yet; as usual mum was the taxi and I had to attend church first. That was the payoff, or I wasn't allowed to go out. Fine then. I'll just get Mac to meet me outside the church then; brilliant idea!!

It was the longest hour for a religious service in history. Stand up, sit down, kneel, Amen, let's go Father, I got a date, and I swear I just heard a bike. Keeping my cool, I finally made it outside, and there he was, to the left of the church door at the end of the carpark was a young, well-built guy, astride a big hunk of a shiny motorbike patiently waiting for the YL…oh my he looked like a proper biker dude, how very rebellious of me.

My heart started to race at the thought of finally meeting the owner of the smooth, deep, sexy voice. Okay, legs, don't get wibbly wobbly. Keep cool body, just casually stroll over and say 'Hi'. Inside, I was a hot mess, in a good way!!!

A short encounter was had that evening with the CB biker named Mac. Perhaps it was for the best, perhaps the angels were looking out for me, or perhaps it was because arranging an eyeball with a hot dude at the front of a church with my mum walking up behind me to introduce herself wasn't such a great idea after all.

Secret No. 6

Scars On The Inside

I was raised in what is considered a normal or average family in the sense that there was my mum, dad and my three older brothers. We had moved here from overseas, so there was no other family here. Dad was kind, gentle and a hard worker, and at times, he worked two jobs to support the family. Until I was about six years old, Mum was a stay-at-home mum, but even when she started working, she was always there when we got home from school.

Although there was no physical affection shown in my family, the way we showed 'affection' was to tease with humour and jokingly put each other down. Looking back, I now think this had a detrimental effect on my sense of self-worth.

We lived pay cheque to pay cheque; neither of my parents drank, gambled, or used drugs, and I never heard them argue. I had no memory of what followed until I met a friend when I was about 22 years old. She told me about her upbringing, and I was shocked, to say the least, when my own suppressed memories surfaced. They are a bit scattered, and the ages might be off, but this is part of my life story.

Secret No. 6: Scars On The Inside

I was about nine years old when my eldest brother started coming into my room at night and sexually abused me. (It took me many years before I called it abuse, as he never hurt me physically or threatened me in any way). I remember fearing the nights, and being sick often.

One time, my brother was hanging out at a neighbour's house with two of his friends, and I wanted to see what they were doing. One of them said I could stay if I bent over and touched my toes. I said, 'You will look up my dress!' They said they wouldn't, but of course they did. One of them asked if I wanted to sit up on the railing around the veranda. I remember my brother saying, 'She is my sister, I'll do it.' He picked me up, put me on the railing and rubbed his hand between my legs.

I ran home, took off my dress, threw it in the bin and refused to wear dresses for many years. I think now it was a protection mechanism. I became a tomboy and not the least bit girly. That didn't stop my brother. I remember I was scared to go to sleep in case I would be woken by my brother touching me, with me unable to move, frozen with fear. I started having regular nightmares, and it was usually the same dream that, as far as I recall, stopped after my brother stopped coming to my room.

I remember being in bed one night, and my brother brought home his first girlfriend. I felt relieved and sure that his night-time visits would stop, but this was not to be the case, so a few more layers of fear, shame and guilt were added. I do not know how many times it happened, or why, and I don't remember exactly when it finally stopped. My parents didn't talk about sex or that it was wrong to be touched inappropriately. I knew it was not nice to hit someone because it could hurt them. I knew of stranger danger, but in my mind, that was a creepy old man with lollies trying to kidnap you. Not my brother.

I wasn't only being abused at home. I wasn't safe at my friend's house either – there was no escape. I was about the same age, nine years old, when my friend's father started touching me. There are a few incidents that stand out.

One time, he took my friend and me to the movies and arranged it so that I was sitting next to him. When the movie started, he put his coat over my lap, and started touching me. I felt the fear again, the same fear that I felt at night when my brother came into my room. I excused myself to go to the toilet, and when I came back, I sat on the other side of my friend, leaving a gap between her dad and us. I became very confused and conflicted - her dad had just sexually assaulted me, but then I was enjoying the movie and ice cream with my friend.

Another time, he had us both barefoot stomping around in a barrel of grapes, crushing them to make wine. We were having so much fun until her dad 'helped' us out of the barrel. Each time he touched me, I felt it was wrong, dirty, and I felt fear. There was worse to come.

Secret No. 6: Scars On The Inside

I can recall the feeling of being frozen with fear, eyes wide open, the heavy weight of his body, the smell of his aftershave, him saying, 'Be a good girl,' as he was on top of me, trying to pull down my pants. Luckily, I heard her mum's voice, and he stopped. It gave me the chance to run away from the house. I caught up with my friend who was on the way to the milk bar with 50 cents, which was a lot for kids back then. I thought she was so lucky, but now I wonder if her dad gave her this money as payment for abuse.

We sat in the sunshine eating sunny boys and lollies, and I felt confused. My body was telling me one thing, run and don't go back, but I was also sad as there had been some fun times in her house with my friend and her family. She was like the sister I never had, but I knew I could not go back again (this would come back to haunt me many years later). I only saw her at school after that.

These memories are not just thoughts in my head. There is a strong physical reaction as well - fear, anxiety, my heart racing and dry retching as I write. However, I'm very pleased to say after writing this story, I no longer have those same physical reactions. Perhaps there has been some healing in writing about what happened to me.

There was another sexual assault when I assumed I had my drink spiked at a party. It was at one of my other brother's parties when I was about 17 years old. I knew everyone there as my brother had known them for years, and I felt safe. I remember one of his friends sitting next to me and giving me a drink, and then I began feeling really weird. I could hardly walk, and he helped me to the spare room. When I woke up the next day, I was half undressed and had a horrible stomach-churning feeling that something terrible had happened, but I put it down to being drunk for the first time.

When all these memories came back to me, I felt dirty, ashamed, used, sad, angry and very alone. I knew I needed help dealing with this, and I found a group therapy class for sexual abuse victims, which I thought would be helpful. I went along, and as I sat with other women and listened to their horrific stories, I thought that what happened to me was not that bad and that I should just forget about it all and get on with life, and I did for many years.

My first boyfriend was a friend of my brother. I was 17, and he was 20. He was the first guy to show an interest in me. It was fairly innocent at first, but within a few months, he was more sexually demanding than I could cope with or wanted. I left after a year.

In my early 20s, I went through the 'bad boy' phase. The first one was a goodish/bad boy who was my first love. He was nice to me but liked his drinking, fighting, and at times, I wouldn't hear from him for days as he was out drinking and doing God knows what. The next one was a bad/bad boy. After ignoring a few red flags, I met his family and friends, and I knew these were not the type of people I wanted in my life. Most of them were in and out of jail; they had addictions of every kind. Taking drugs, people of all states of drunkenness, swearing and threats of violence

Secret No. 6: Scars On The Inside

seemed the norm for both the men and women, and all of this with kids around.

I decided then that I didn't want to be in this relationship anymore, but a few days later, I found out I was pregnant. When I told him, he threw his arm in the air and walked away saying, 'Do whatever you want, but I'm having nothing to do with it.'

For many reasons, at 22 years of age, I decided to terminate my pregnancy. A few days later, I thought the father still had the right to know. When I saw him, I said, 'I'm not pregnant anymore.' He replied, 'Good!!! Now fuck off!!' I walked away (I know what a charmer, Huh). I remember thinking, 'Phew, lucky I dodged a bullet with that one.' The last I heard, he had been in and out of jail and had four kids to three women. I got on with life and was doing a fairly good job at it.

This was until I met a lady who was into all things spiritual. We chatted, and I mentioned that I had had several sexual abuse encounters in my life. We talked for a bit, and she asked me if I had ever had a healing done. My first reply was, 'Nah, all good. That was years ago, and it doesn't bother me anymore.' But she understood how we could subconsciously hold onto the past, and we talked about it for a while. I thought this was interesting and agreed to have a healing session with her.

I was amazed at what came out during this session. I cried like I had never cried before. It came from somewhere deep inside of me, and then up came the anger. I felt sick to my stomach but comfortable enough to let it all out (or so I thought). One surprising emotion I felt was guilt. I held onto so much guilt about my friend when I realised her dad had been giving her 50 cents regularly after molesting her, and that I had left her alone to be abused by her father and that I could have somehow stopped it from happening (which I know is not true).

I composed myself and thanked her very much, and as I was leaving, she suggested I come back for another session. I said I would but didn't, as I had another idea. I thought that I'd confront my brother and let him know I remembered what he did. I felt that this would help me heal, so I wrote him a letter. When we met up in a park a few days later to discuss what had happened, he did not apologise. He listened to what I had to say, then said he didn't remember any of it and said, 'Don't tell our parents.'

I hated, resented and avoided being near him for years, at times missing family events because I couldn't deal with being around him, but only having six family members living in Australia, I wanted them around, so I avoided him as much as I could.

Life went on. I met a man at work, and we started a relationship. A year later, when I gave birth to my beautiful daughter, the amount of unresolved crap that came up surprised me, and I felt the need to let my parents know what my brother had done to me. I'm not sure what I expected; maybe a hug and some sympathy, but neither of these happened. My dad walked past, patted me on the head, and left the room.

have to be cross-examined. He got the maximum sentence allowed, eight years, although part of me still thinks his sentence is not long enough. I am blessed and grateful that I have great friends who supported us every step of the way. The silver lining in all of this is that my daughter and I became closer than I could have ever imagined, and I am proud that she calls me her rock.

I thought I was finished with abusive men, but unfortunately, this wasn't the case. After a few years, I met a new man, and after dating for a couple of months, he became verbally and emotionally abusive. When I ended the relationship with him, he started harassing me, constantly calling and texting me up to 100 times a day. He broke into my house and stole a few very sentimental items, targeting these because he knew the emotional story behind them. He also removed all the fuses from the fuse box and went through my underwear drawer, which really creeped me out. He would sit in his car out the front of the house for hours at night.

I became very fearful for both my daughter and my safety. This happened for months, and I hoped he would just stop, but in the end, I had to go to the police and then court to get an AVO, which, luckily for us, was the end of his harassment.

After my daughter was born, I started having uncomfortable periods, but following my daughter's sexual abuse, my gynaecological problems got worse. I suffered from endometriosis, fibroids and occasionally, ovarian cysts. Sometimes, the pain and bleeding would have me in bed for two or three days, and there were a few trips to the hospital. Some months, I would have PMS for a week, then bleed for a week or more, and then feel washed out for another week after, so that for three out of four weeks in a month, I was unwell.

A healer I attended picked up on my problem without me telling her about it and told me that I needed to release and heal old emotions. If I worked on releasing my emotions, the intensity of my pain would lessen for a while, but it was short-lived. The issues and pain returned.

After ten years of seeing many doctors and being prescribed countless different medications, one of which had particularly bad side effects, and investigative surgery confirming the mess my uterus was in, I had a hysterectomy. I have never looked back; it is one of the best things I did, but I do believe that if I understood how our bodies hold onto old painful emotions and how to heal them, then maybe I could have avoided having my gynaecological problems and needing the hysterectomy.

I also learnt to be mindful of what you are thinking and saying to yourself. I had a bad habit of constantly saying, 'I'm sick and tired' of this or that, and guess what? I was sick and tired a lot!

I often wondered if I would ever trust another man enough to be in another relationship again. I have had many healings done over the years, and with the understanding of how they work, that I need to work on myself, and that healing is an ongoing process, I no longer hold onto anger and resentment against the people who had hurt me in the past. We are all here in this life to learn and go through our own stuff and learn our own lessons. I have now been in a wonderful relationship for seven years.

As I mentioned, healing is an ongoing process, and I have new stuff to work on. There were many fazes where I didn't want to have anything to do with spirituality because I thought if there was a God and we had guardian angels, then mine had done a terrible job at helping, guiding or protecting me, but this is not the case. I was not listening to my intuition, and I was not paying attention. I was not doing the hard work; I was not grateful for all the good in my life.

While I was writing this story, my daughter told me she was pregnant. I am happy and excited about being a grandmother, but a feeling came up that was very unexpected. Part of me hoped for a boy, because a boy would not have to go through what both me and my daughter have been through.

I felt sad and disappointed that this feeling came up, but now I'm aware of it, I can start working on the next chapter of my story, to heal and move forward with peace, for myself, my daughter and future generations because what WE think, feel and how we behave has a knock-on effect on those around us.

I would like to thank Lisa for this opportunity to not only write my story for her book, but for me to purge and heal. At first, I wondered if my story was worthy of telling, but I thought if it helps one person, then it is a good thing. It turns out that writing this has helped me to get rid of long-held baggage.

If you are thinking about writing your own story, say 'YES'. Your story matters. It could be the story that changes someone's life (even if it is just your own). At times, it was difficult. At times, I had to stop writing as I felt physically sick as old wounds came up. There were sleepless nights, waking up in the middle of the night, remembering things and needing to write them down straight away.

But it has been cathartic in releasing long-held painful thoughts, beliefs and feelings, and I am so glad to be sharing my story with you.

Secret No. 7

My Journey So Far

I hope that by reading this chapter, you may feel inspired to live your life to the fullest and learn to love yourself unconditionally.

I was born in Launceston, Tasmania, in April 1952, the second eldest child to a Czechoslovakian father and a mother who was German of English descent. I had three younger siblings, altogether we were two sisters and two brothers. My father had many mental issues, possibly because of his harsh upbringing and being seconded to a German armaments factory in the Second World War, but despite its harsh environment, he managed to get his training as a mechanical engineer. He arrived in Tasmania just after the war.

He had violent and extreme mood swings, plus he was an alcoholic, undiagnosed from an early age, and he really didn't want to have children. I don't remember, but my mother told me that as a baby, he used to spank me so much that I would scream every time I saw him, which resulted in him hitting me even more. My brother, who was one and a half years older than me, received the same sort of abuse; however, it didn't seem to scare him as much. Possibly, as a result of this abuse, I never crawled; I only ever slid around on my backside, maybe because it made me more aware of what was going on around me.

Despite the early childhood violence I received from my father, I have never hated him or anyone else. Especially as I got older, I realised that he was responding and acting in accordance with his own upbringing. Despite this understanding, this and other abuse, which I will touch on soon, caused many emotional hang-ups and fears throughout my teenage and early adult years.

My mother separated from him when I was about two years old; however, I managed to maintain a relationship with him and occasionally stayed with him and his new wife during some school holiday periods. Unfortunately, as a result of his continual abuse of his body with alcohol, he died when he was about 60 years old. I was the only one of his children to mum who attended his funeral in Brisbane.

My mother was born in Sydney in 1923. She was the second eldest of four children. Not long after she was born, her mother and father moved to Nietta, Tasmania, where, despite her father also being a severe alcoholic, they managed to buy a small farm property.

Unfortunately for Mum and her brothers, they lived a very subsistence-level life, eventually being taken by the rich aunt and uncle to live and work on their potato farm at Forth on the northwest coast of Tasmania. These days this couple would be considered very cruel; there was much physical violence if they didn't do their many chores before and after school. In addition, very abusive nuns ran the school that they were attending. I guess this made Mum very tough, but also very affectionate.

She worked hard all her life and managed to stay with her abusive husband, my father, for over four years. Despite being tough, she always tried to be kind and, as I said, affectionate. Before she met her second husband, she fell in love with an Italian man, and they had a child together who was adopted out at birth.

Because of the shame she felt, I never learned about him until I was about 34. He and his wife found us, and while we lived in different states, we became very close. They had one child together, who is my youngest sister. I am very close to all my siblings, especially my two youngest sisters. Her children always loved Mum dearly until her passing at age 96. Unfortunately, she suffered from dementia for the last ten years of her life because of eight mini-strokes she had, which are known to kill brain cells.

Mum's second husband was also a mentally disturbed man who had major issues with alcohol, coupled with a very quick and violent temper, not to Mum, but to me. It was not uncommon for him to get angry and kick me up the backside or punch me in the face if I forgot to do something or didn't do it to his liking.

This happened until I was in my teenage years. When I was about 11 years old, I decided I would run away from home because I did not want to put up with any more of this abuse.

We were living in Launceston at the time, and Mum and my step-father were caretakers at a private Christian school. I was meant to go to school that day but decided to walk 150 km away to stay with my step-grandmother, who I felt loved me and made me feel special. She lived at St Helens on the northeast coast and was instrumental in having us baptised Catholics as children. Whenever we lived at St Helens, she would always insist on us going to church with her. Because of her influence, I thought I would become a Catholic priest, but I realised as I got older that it was not my calling.

I got within 25 km of her house but was seen by drivers who reported me. The police were suspicious of my story that I was going to visit my grandmother, and decided to leave me at the St Mary's police station and contacted my mother and step-father. As you can imagine, after having to drive from Launceston to collect me, they were very angry, especially my father, who decided to punch me many times in the face and torso. We stopped at my step-grandmother's that night. I remember my grandmother being very empathetic and comforting me.

Because of my behaviour, Mum and my step-father decided to let my step-uncle and aunt take me to live on their pig farm. As they only had three daughters, they thought it would be handy to have a boy to help with all the physical work, but unfortunately for them, I did not live up to their expectations. After about three months, they decided to send me back home.

Mum and my step-father were still caretakers at a private school, so they tried to send me back to the Catholic primary school, but they would not forgive me for not turning up on the day that I ran away from home, so instead, I was sent to a public school to finish my primary education.

I should say at this stage, that another possible cause for my early insecurities was the fact that from the age of four until I left home when I was 15, my step-father and mum moved to a total of 96 different jobs. So, just after I returned home, they moved back to a farm in the country. My sister and I used to travel about 30 km a day to and from school, and I was bullied every day, which seemed to happen for most of my school life, except when I went to St Helens State School. I was in Grade 8 there and managed to make a couple of good friends. Possibly also because the headmaster, who was also our teacher, took a real shine to me and encouraged my learning. In fact, I used to get teased that I was his pet.

Before we moved back to St Helens, my parents worked on a farm near Longford. It was expected that I would also help on the farm before and after school, helping to milk about 150 cows with an old milking machine. We would be out there at 5.30 am and then again at 4.00 pm when I got home from school.

During this time, at age 13, I learned to drive my first tractor and eventually my first car on the road, which my step-father taught me out of possible need because he was blind in one eye and only had 17% vision in the other. He managed to drive most of his life by borrowing his best friend's license. Obviously, at that age, I was way too young, but I think he and Mum thought it was the lesser of the two evils, so I became his driver until I left home.

After about six months on this farm, we moved again to another farm nearby. During this time, I was sometimes sent back to the previous residence to stay with my parents' friends and help on their farm. My parents trusted them, but they shouldn't have.

All of the men in that family decided to take advantage of me and sexually abuse me. They stripped me, held me captive and masturbated me. While there was a part of me that felt totally disgusted, I must be honest and say there was also another part of me that enjoyed the experience. This, of course, caused me to feel very guilty, especially given my deep religious convictions. I did tell my parents about this, but I'm not sure that they totally believed me; however, although they did remain friends, they never sent me back there again.

The last year and a half of my schooling was spent at St Helens State School because my parents moved back to the area. This was about the fifth time we lived in the district. During part of this time, we lived in a rundown old house without power or running water, which was owned by a farmer about eight km from St Helen's township.

Within a very short time, he asked whether I would come and work for him after school and during school holidays, which I was happy to do, even though my pay was only $0.20 an hour.

As time went by, we became very close friends, and apart from my headmaster, he became more like a mentor, and I remained very close to him and his wife until they passed many years ago. It was hard work doing a whole mix of all duties, including milking cows, feeding up and clearing land. After about six months, he doubled my income to $0.40 an hour. I managed to buy my first pushbike and camera with this money.

I have always had a passion for singing and photography and still do to this day. In fact, photography became my main source of income for the last years of my working life, and I still take professional photos, mostly on-location portraiture, in many areas of Australia, especially between South Australia and Tasmania.

Singing runs in the family; Mum, my real father, step-father and two sisters all sang, with my youngest sister being a well-known country music singer, musician, and songwriter. To further my love of singing, I decided to seek out a classical voice trainer who was an amazingly talented and patient tutor. I spent six years under her guidance and increased my range from one and a half octaves to four.

I have digressed. After my schooling at St Helens, my parents moved back to Launceston. They did not value education, so they decided to get me a job at age 14 at the car yard detailing cars. However, that didn't last too long because, as a result of my love of riding pushbikes, I was involved in a collision with a car. The driver, who did not see me, hit me and knocked me off, which resulted in a very badly broken leg. I was in plaster from my toes to the top of my leg for over ten weeks.

Although I was very shy and timid at this age, as no one was at home, I would go for long walks on my crutches; people would often engage me in conversation, which I loved. I also spent quite a lot of time sketching cityscapes; this was a continuation of my favourite subject at school, which was technical drawing.

A short time after I was out of plaster, we moved to Burnie on the northwest coast. Once again, my parents worked on a farm just outside the small city. When I was able to walk, I acquired employment detailing cars for a Rent-A-Car company. I was 15 when I started, and I stayed there for nearly three years.

Because of my step-grandmother's influence, I stayed loyal to the Catholic Church, where I met some great young people older than me, who invited me to join their youth group. One young man who was the president became my first real mentor, and as a result of his caring and nurturing attitude, he influenced me to start reading positive psychology books, my first being *How To Stop Worrying and Start Living* by Dale Carnegie. This was also my first experience with a form of counselling.

We used to visit hospitals and look for patients who seemed lonely, and if they wanted, we would engage them in conversation.

While involved in this youth group, I met my first girlfriend. While I had a wish to find a nice girl previously, I was too shy and scared, and because I feared rejection, I didn't ask anybody out. We dated for three years.

In the beginning, her parents, who were quite conservative, seemed to like me, but as time went on, I believe they thought we were getting too serious, so they took a dislike to me and our relationship and tried to break us up. Unfortunately for them, it only encouraged us to continue our relationship, including our first sexual experience.

Regrettably, as we were starting to grow apart, we found that she was pregnant. Despite her parent's strict Catholicism, they wanted her to get an abortion, which was nearly impossible in those days. When the child was born, it was given for adoption. All I knew was that it was a girl, and she would be now about 45. Obviously, I would love to meet her if I ever find out that she is looking for her biological parents. Just before she was born, we separated.

Not long after we broke up, I was living in Launceston, working for a supermarket bulk store. I transferred my membership from Burnie to re-join the youth group, where I met my next girlfriend. After 12 months, when we were both 21, we decided to get married. I would say, looking back, that we were both very needy, but in our own way, we loved each other and given that we were both practising Catholics at the time, it lasted for 35 years. After we broke up, we went through a grieving process that we helped each other through, and we have remained good friends to this day.

During our time together, while we did not have much in common, we had a mutual love of children and wanted a large family. We had seven of our own, three girls and four boys, and we also adopted my youngest sister's child at 17 months. We loved him as our own, but he was always aware that he was my sister's child. I was the only father figure he knew, but he recognised that my ex-wife and sister were like two mothers, and he says to this day that he was very privileged. He has a very similar talent to my sister in relation to music and is a talented vocalist and musician.

We feel very blessed that all our children are mostly doing what they want with their lives. We now have seven grandchildren. I would say that we are a close and affectionate family, despite the fact that I now live in South Australia. For the last 14 years, we have been in regular contact, and I usually visit Tasmania every three to four months. Obviously, that has decreased a little since Covid 19. We endeavour to have a family gathering during most of my visits, and I get the privilege of staying with them and my two sisters on many occasions.

At the end of all my years of being married and rearing children, plus my research, study, and reading of positive psychology and mental health, I was able to help my ex search online dating sites. I was very helpful to her as I have quite a high profile in Tasmania because of my involvement in the community and photographing many large functions, including the Launceston Royal show, political gatherings, Crime Stoppers functions, carnivals, the yearly Launceston Cup, fashions on the field and numerous civic functions. I knew and was able to advise her on possible suitors. As it turned out, the man she originally married I did not know at all, but I am happy that she found a wonderful man who is better suited to her than I ever was.

In reference to my work a few years before I met my first wife, after working at the Rent-A-Car firm for three years, I decided a slight change would be interesting, so I procured a job, still detailing cars for a new and used car company. After six months and a very short time working for a door-to-door sewing machine business in Launceston, working for a boss who was extremely verbally abusive, I decided to work for the supermarket bulk store that I mentioned earlier.

I did this work for about four months, then applied for work selling Ford cars spare parts and accessories for a major car company, which gave me some in-house training. This company's owner could see a lot of potential in me, as I had gained a lot of confidence through the youth group, plus practising many of the concepts I was learning from my ongoing research into positive mental health and psychology. They intended for my long-term position to be selling new and used cars when I was old enough, but unfortunately, there was a downturn in the Australian economy, and I was retrenched.

Secret No. 7: My Journey So Far

I was still with my first long-term girlfriend during this time. I decided then to start working for Electrolux, selling vacuum cleaners door-to-door, which I did very successfully without working very hard. One of the gentlemen who bought a vacuum cleaner from me owned a local sewing machine shop, and he took a shine to my attitude and said that if I ever wanted to work for him, he would be happy to employ me. So, after 12 months with Electrolux, I decided to take him up on his offer.

It was around this time that my long-term girlfriend and I separated. The owner of this business and I became very close personal friends, and he became another mentor. I worked with him for 20 years. During the company's best time, we had a team of ten. I learned everything that you could possibly know about the sewing machine industry, from selling them door-to-door, in-store selling and marketing, plus repairing and servicing them. Eventually, we became partners because he allowed me to buy into the business.

In the last two years that I worked there, my partner decided to take a job working for an overseas charity, so he left me to run the whole business. During the last two years, I also ventured out on my own, opening a new sewing machine shop in Burnie. Eventually, the shop in Launceston was sold, so I opened a new one in a suburb of Launceston called Kings Meadows. I owned two shops for approximately two years until I could see the writing on the wall and was starting to lose a lot of money. In hindsight, it would have served me to have closed them sooner because, eventually, the losses were too great, and I was bankrupted.

My financial backstop during all these years was a portrait, wedding, and function photography business, which, after I closed the sewing businesses, became my full-time work and income. Much of the photography business was on location; however, I owned a studio. In addition, my then-wife and I would travel into country areas, setting up studios, and doing makeovers for clients, with before and after shots. According to the industry, we were consistently doing more photography than anyone else in the state.

As if I was not busy enough, I met another wonderful man and his wife, who ran a very successful Amway business. He asked me to join him, and for several years, we were moderately successful. Still, in my opinion, it was a great learning opportunity, introducing me to many more positive psychology books and inspirational people. He became a lifelong friend and mentor, honouring me and my now wife by being my best man for our wedding in Adelaide eight years ago.

You may remember earlier, I mentioned that I was helping my first wife with dating sites. By this stage in my life, I believe I had learned the concept of loving myself unconditionally, so I was very secure and happy in my own skin, and I knew that I would be happy whether I was in or out of a relationship. But being a romantic at heart, I thought this would be great fun to meet some new people of the opposite sex. Plus, because by this time, I had been meditating for over

20 years, I had become a strong believer, through personal experience, that whatever we most think about, especially with passion, we will manifest. So, with this thinking, I wrote and envisioned who would be my ideal partner. As a result of this thinking, I thought the first person I made friends with on one of these apps would become my long-term girlfriend, but whilst we have remained good friends, those feelings were not reciprocated. But I didn't lose hope; after meeting a few more ladies online and in person, I eventually met the love of my life, my best friend and soulmate, who lived in Adelaide.

After talking on social media and the phone for a few months, she decided to visit me in Launceston. So before we even met, even if there weren't any pheromones in common or any romantic attraction, we knew we were going to be good friends.

As it turned out, there was a very strong connection between us. We travelled backwards and forwards for 12 months. Given that my partner's position at a private rehabilitation Hospital was permanent, we decided it would be easier for me to move to Adelaide, and I haven't ever regretted it as I am blessed to be able to travel to Tasmania to visit family and friends on a regular basis, dependent of course on Covid 19 restrictions.

Eight years ago, we decided to get married. From a personal point of view, moving to Adelaide and marrying were the two best decisions I have ever made. I consider myself so blessed to be living and sharing my life with such a wonderful person.

Wanting to make a more significant impact in Australia and the wider world, I decided at age 58 to take my research into mental health to another level, so I enrolled through the Australian College of Applied Psychology to complete a degree in counselling and coaching.

I loved my time there, learning new ideas, and spending wonderful times getting to know some great lecturers and fellow students. However, not wanting to seem immodest, given my years of experience, research, and study, I had lecturers acknowledge that they were unaware of some of the concepts I had learned over all those years. But I must say I learned much more from them than they did from me.

I have continued counselling and coaching clients through my not-for-profit service, one-on-one, by phone and online. After all these years of research, study and anecdotally, I have concluded that the most important lesson we all need to learn is how to love ourselves unconditionally.

In fact, over 95% of the world population lacks ideal self-esteem, so in March 2021, I recorded my first webinar. Whilst it hasn't gone viral yet, I have had a few thousand people watch it so far, with many glowing reports. I intend to present public workshops in this area and hopefully, a Ted Talk, combining it with an inspirational song at the beginning and the end because I believe music is so powerful in touching souls and emotions.

Secret No. 8

Finding My Voice

December 1981

'If a man hits you, leave'. My mother's words echo through my brain as I wake to a fist in my face, blood from my nose oozing down my front. Shocked, I get up and walk out the door and drive home. Within minutes, the phone is ringing. It is him with his profound apology, 'It will never happen again!' he says. I drive back to him. That is my first mistake. We spend a day or so talking about what happened. He didn't mean it, he said. 'I saw you talking to a man at the party,' he said. 'I was drunk,' he said. All words, but I go back.

It is three months into our torrid relationship. He is full-on. He asked me to marry him two weeks after we met. Red flags, I know, but I ignore these. I'm in love. Here is a man who 'loves' me like no man ever has. It is wild, it is scary, and it seems real.

Once you have been hit, though, a certain fear comes over you. You are never the same again. There's the fear of him getting drunk and causing a scene at social events, the walking on eggshells, the wondering how he is going to be when you pick him up drunk at 2.00 am. Did I just see him kicking an old man on the footpath? Ignore, ignore, survive, survive. The shame! I am an educated woman, a feminist no less, who believes in equality and the ideals of being kind to other humans. What to do?

When he isn't drunk or high or visiting other women, he is charming, articulate, funny and creative. We read together. We learn together, and we plan our life together. What shall we call our first baby? We hold an engagement champagne breakfast so he can meet my family. Mum, when told we were to be married, says, 'You don't think you're being a little impetuous, do you?' I have to look the word up. Impetuous – acting or done quickly without thought or care. Impulsive, rash, hasty, reckless. Yes, that's me. 'But he loves me,' I retort.

September, 1982

The wedding invitations are posted that afternoon. I am in bed and wake with a fist in my stomach. The punches are coming fast and furious. I pretend to be dead. Maybe that will stop him. I'm not sure what happened next, but I find myself running barefoot out my front door and up the main street, stopping at the Post Office briefly at 3.00 am to ring the recorded number to engage a substitute teacher for the next day. Ever the thinker and the organiser, I managed to grab 30 cents for the payphone on my way out the door! I keep running and end up at a friend's house nearby. There is no way I'm knocking on his door.

Luckily, my friend has a chair on his front veranda, where I sit for maybe two hours. I thought that's probably enough time for my fiancé to pass out from the alcohol he has copiously consumed.

The next day, the day off I'd organised with that 30 cents, bruised and sore, I call Lifeline. A counselling session is set up for that afternoon. When he is asked how he feels about what he has done, my fiancé cries as he tells them about hitting me. Those tears get to me, and I soften once again. 'He won't do it again,' I tell myself. Some counselling is set up, but he doesn't attend the first appointment or any other appointments that are made for him over the next few years.

The next few years? I hear you ask. Yes. I stay. He is living with me now. One night, he is drunk, and I threaten to leave. Picture this. I am in my car in the driveway, ready to drive off, when suddenly there he is, naked and jumping on the car bonnet, like Spiderman, yelling and pleading for me to stay! The horror of 'what will the neighbours think' reverberates through my being as I finally manage to get away.

I drive to a 7/11, buy myself a hot chocolate and some smokes and park in a shopping centre car park on a hill overlooking Melbourne for a couple of hours in the middle of the night. Later, I creep back in and still manage to turn up to school the next day with my 'I'm OK' mask firmly in place. There is a constant reminder of that bizarre night in the form of a permanent dent in my almost-new car bonnet.

Secret No. 8: Finding My Voice

He gains a promotion to train as a computer operator with the Commonwealth Government in Canberra. At this stage, I cannot stand the idea of us being apart, so I apply for the now-defunct spouse leave from the Education Department. We marry and move to Canberra in late 1982. I am 27 years old.

March 1983

'I've left him, Mum.' I stand at my mother's front door, having put all the wedding presents in the car and driven eight hours from Canberra to Melbourne. 'Take her to the pub for a drink,' my mother commands my sister. 'Your brother and sister-in-law are coming for dinner in an hour. You're just having a little holiday.' I'm not able to tell her that he's been with another woman and is possibly using heroin. My silence is screaming at me, and it seems I am also silenced by my mother. The shame, the fear, the confusion. Have a drink and forget about it. Push the emotions down. Put on a good face. So I do. The flowers arrive the next day, the apologies begin again, and I drive back to Canberra.

Living with the fear and uncertainty of his erratic behaviour becomes my norm. I push through my anxiety and enrol in a writing course. I write and perform a protest song about the Franklin River Dam. Bob Hawke is elected, and the river is saved. I write about my fear of birds, especially magpies. In Canberra, the magpies seem particularly territorial, and my walks with my husband have me with my head tucked firmly into his arm or, on one particular day, crawling along a path near Parliament House with my handbag on my head, pleading, 'Please, Mrs Magpie, leave me alone; I'm not going to hurt your babies.' People in Canberra construct elaborate adornments on their bike helmets.

I gain a teaching job, and we wear helmets on yard duty! I am terrified as a memory comes flooding back – I'm a teenager, walking through a park and – whoosh - what was that? A magpie draws blood in my pigtails' perfect part. Push that fear down, not allowed to have emotions, have another drink. At this stage, I don't know any other way. There are good times still, and mostly our marriage works within the framework of my mind. He applies for a job in Melbourne.

1984

Things are running smoothly, it seems. The emphasis is on the word 'seems'. We join a community group, People for Nuclear Disarmament, and make new friends. I am teaching at my old school, and he has a job requiring shift work, which suits us both. I notice a belt in the bathroom cupboard. What's that for? Is that used for hitting up?

Am I so naïve, or do I choose to ignore it? We've found a beer that has a low alcohol count. I buy him slabs of that. I still remember the name, Swan Lager, from Western Australia. I should have bought shares in the company! I'm thinking if he doesn't get drunk, he'll be okay. I notice furtive looks between him and one of the women in our group, but I choose to ignore it. When he is with me, life seems okay.

Over the next two years, we throw ourselves into the creativity of the group, organising and taking part in some peaceful protests, airbrushing t-shirts and bottling wine to raise funds. We join 200,000 people on the Palm Sunday Rallies in Melbourne. We join the organising committee of a two-week peace camp to be held in a Melbourne suburb near a satellite dish we believe to be a communications signal for the US nuclear war machine. We connect with politicians. We take part in International Year of Peace activities.

We love our newfound group. We laugh and learn together, share meals, joints and lots of wine. I'm living in the bliss of these times but am ignorant to my husband's underlying activities.

1986

Ten weeks into the year at a new school, I am discharged from my teaching position on extended stress leave, under the guise of back pain, which, in effect, is the result of extreme stress and anxiety. I've been shoving this down, more often than not, with copious amounts of alcohol. He is working shifts, so we are often 'ships in the night'.

I am sitting at my mother's one evening at 5.00 pm, and she remarks, 'Aren't you going home to get his tea ready?' Infuriated, I bite back, 'He knows how to cook,' thinking I am an enlightened woman who won't have a man dictate my hours. In reality, I am confused, anxious, angry and unsettled, and my life seems to be in tatters.

June 1986

'Are you doing some renovations?' the bank manager inquires on an unexpected phone call. 'No, why?' is my quizzical and quavering reply. 'Lately, one hundred dollars is being withdrawn from your joint credit card account every day.' My heart drops to my stomach. How would I ever repay two and a half thousand dollars? That's a lot of money in 1986.

Upon checking, the same ATM in Brunswick Street Fitzroy is being accessed each day. My mind is racing. 'That's one of Melbourne's hotspots for heroin, isn't it?' I ask myself, knowing full well the answer. My instincts tell me the truth. How did I not see this coming? What do I do? Who do I tell? I tell no one.

The shame and taboo of heroin use is huge in my mind. The same shame, that shame of the secrecy of abuse, whirls inside me like a demon to be hushed. Once again, I silence myself. How can I tell someone? What will they think of me? If I tell, I'll have to do something about it.

To top it off, my suspicions of him conducting a relationship with that other woman in our group are realised. I confront him, and he denies it. 'But I love you', he says, 'I married you,' he says. I confront her. 'What did HE say?' she asks. Aha! These were the only words I needed. It WAS true. The looks, the not coming home, the excuses, the lies; these and more come tumbling in as I am finally defeated. I very quietly help him pack and move him out and into her

Secret No. 8: Finding My Voice

house. I go to my parents and finally tell them about his abuse. Enough. It is over.

How did I manage to be so quiet, so nice, so accommodating?

For almost 35 years, I'd believed that my self-esteem was so low that I attracted someone who would abuse me. This belief helped me to understand the inner torture of 'Why did this happen to me?' and it helped me on my inner journey to self-love. I believed that I had to take responsibility for what happened to me. I believed it was my fault.

I spent years pursuing spiritual studies, past lives, and all sorts of weird and wonderful concepts and beliefs in the hope I might understand myself and make sense of my life. And it did, to an extent. It helped me to survive, but I truly felt there was something very wrong with me.

Recently, when speaking about this story to a good friend, she reflected, 'You've always been a loving, generous person, H. You didn't deserve any of that.' It hit me like a ton of bricks, and the self-blame began to lift.

Some anger crept in, as did the stark realisation. That's it! As long as a woman keeps silent, as long as she has no voice with her peers, her family, or even with the police, then a woman will continue to be murdered every week in Australia. We must have courage and speak up. We must teach our children that it's safe to tell. We must look for signs in our friends. That's a tricky one, as often, the abused woman just isn't ready or doesn't want to confront the truth.

In my case, it was the silence, the deep shame and the fear to speak up. It was my denial and the pushing down of my emotions to 'not tell'. This was learnt when I was sexually abused as a four-year-old and told, 'If you tell, you're dead!' I'd lived my life so scared, so anxious on the inside, while on the outside, I was social and gregarious and loved by many.

My mind was so powerful that it even pushed the sexual abuse far down, enough to survive, covered up for over 35 years. It eventually surfaced in my 40s once I had the tools to deal with it. But that's another story.

Back to 1986, when I go to my parents, him finally kicked out and ensconced in his new abode, and me laying everything out on the table, my mother, with such compassion, says, 'You deserve an Academy Award, my love. Out of all my children, I thought you were the happiest. I'm so sorry those things happened to you.'

Secret No. 9

Life Is What You Make It

Have you ever had a deep and meaningful and asked yourself the question, 'What is my purpose in life?' There is no doubt life throws us curveballs from time to time, and we all know our lives are subjective, which is why I always like to connect and soul search within myself, to enable me to stay grounded, appreciative and grateful for every day I share with you on this earth.

I was born in Manchester, England; I'd like to take you back to before I was born, right to this present day, sharing with you not only my story, my purpose and my view of life, but to offer hope and love to each person who can relate, or may relate one day, to the experiences I share.

It was early August in 1982, my father, excitedly awaiting what would have undoubtedly been the second proudest day of his life, after marrying the love of his life. He was about to become a father for the first time. A perfectly healthy, precious gift of life was weeks away from being born, and the excitement of finally finding out whether he would be gifted with a son or daughter.

With only a few weeks to go, his wife was taken to hospital due to complications with the pregnancy. Unfortunately, she had high blood pressure as a result of preeclampsia and was admitted for the remainder of her pregnancy.

Days rolled into a week, and then two; my father regularly visited the hospital to be by his wife and unborn child's side until the day came when the doctors made the decision on August 26th, 1982, to induce due to her preeclampsia and concerns for the baby's wellbeing.

Due to further complications through the labour, the doctors made the decision to perform an emergency caesarean section. She was rushed down to theatre, and my father was ushered into the hospital corridor, where he stayed for four hours waiting for the news on the wellbeing of his wife and the birth of his child. Meanwhile, my father made the phone calls to the family on the hospital payphone and waited patiently for an update from the hospital staff, which didn't come.

The corridor was empty, with no staff around to offer an update, apart from two crash teams that went flying past him. Shortly after, my nana and grandad arrived to offer support, just as my father was being given an update by a passing doctor, who was shocked that he hadn't even been told whether he had a son or daughter.

The image of the two crash teams flooded my father's mind as the doctor's words rolled off his tongue. 'Your wife suffered a cardiac arrest on the operating table. Doctors were able to stabilise her before moving on to your daughter; your wife has been taken to intensive care, and your daughter is about to be taken to another hospital for specialist care.'

My father and nana ran through the hospital to the intensive care baby unit and, by pure luck, made it just in time to see my sister being ushered into an ambulance.

Over the next two days, my father walked to two different hospitals, totalling an 11.8km round trip to see both his wife and his daughter. On August 29th, 1982, my father, who was staying with a friend for moral support, received a phone call from the police telling him he was required to be at Withington Hospital where his wife was. Luckily, his friend could drive him to be by her side.

On the way to the hospital, every traffic light turned red, and every minute felt like a whole hour. When he arrived at the hospital, he was told that his wife had sadly passed away ten minutes before he arrived.

My father and his wife had run a Spiritualist Church in Whalley Range, Manchester, England and had faith in the afterlife. Dad took the continuous red traffic lights as a sign that his wife didn't want him to see her deterioration as she was passing and wanted to pass privately, but nonetheless, he was understandably devastated at the loss of the love of his life.

The next day, August 30th, 1982, when he was visiting his daughter, the hospital chaplain baptised her, and the very next day, on 31st August 1982, her life support was turned off. My sister took one breath on her own and sadly passed away, returning to her mother's loving arms in the afterlife.

My father arranged for his wife and daughter to be placed in the same casket, and they were cremated together, and their ashes scattered on a rose bush in a garden of remembrance.

Four months after they passed, my father was at a service in the spiritualist church. He received a message from the medium who was on the church platform that night. He was given confirmation of the passing of his late wife and daughter and was told he would have another child.

It was now some time in 1985; three years had passed since my father lost his wife and daughter. He was helping a woman who was having paranormal issues in her home, and they became close and formed a relationship. In January of 1986, she fell pregnant with his child. That March, they married before the birth, and on October 4th, 1986, my father was gifted with his second daughter, me.

My father was the first to hold me. He said I had great head control, and he took one look at my mother and said, 'She's been here before.' To which I stuck my tongue out at him, which actually sums me and my personality to this day up to a T.

I truly believe and take comfort in the knowledge that I was chosen, with the blessing from his first wife, to be my father's daughter. I'm not his first daughter, but I am most certainly part of her, as she is part of me. My father had no further children, making me his only living child, and I truly believe part of my purpose in life is to live life for the two of us. Not out of guilt because I'm alive and my sister isn't, but because I believe I was chosen for a reason, which gives me a heart-warming sense of pride and purpose to be the best person I can be with my sister always at the heart of my subconscious being.

My father and I have always been close since the day I were born. With every obstacle life has thrown our way, they have made us closer, and the bond we have is truly unbreakable. When I turned seven years of age, my parents' marriage was breaking down. I was placed into foster care by my mother, who told my father it was for the best whilst they tried to work on their marriage, so he reluctantly agreed.

In the end, the marriage didn't work out, and my mother found my father a two-bedroom unit without his knowledge and sent him on his way. My mother wanted me to be adopted, but my father, who had already lost one daughter, wasn't prepared to allow it to happen again. It took him ten months of fighting the legal system before he finally won full custody of me. I am forever grateful to that Judge.

To celebrate, my father took me to an Indian restaurant, and I was given a single rose, eight chocolate mints and a bowl of ice cream from the staff as a gift for our celebration. I was eight years old, and I remember it like it was yesterday.

Life from that point for me and my father was difficult. My father did anything and everything in his power to make sure I was looked after, and always put me first, working endlessly to provide for me the best he could. We relied heavily on hand-me-downs and kind gestures due to the marital debt my father was left with. I had to grow up much faster than my years, but I truly wouldn't change one thing about my life growing up, despite the hard challenges we faced, the rejection from my mother or the bullying I faced from other children.

I dropped out of high school in Grade Eight due to severe bullying and never went back. I got into a relationship at the age of 13 with a 19-year-old man. I moved in with him and his parents by the age of 15. At the age of 16, I got my very first commission unit. I lived there on my own until I fell pregnant with my first child at the age of 18, and her father moved in with us.

When I was 20, my father was diagnosed with a tumour on his brain. The tumour was the size of an egg, it had cracked his skull with the pressure, and he was left with a metal plate as part of his skull, but thankfully, the tumour was benign, and my father eventually made a full recovery. Not long after that, and around the time of my 21st birthday, I started to see life differently. I left my relationship of eight years and spent the next few months being reckless, spending money on myself, going to parties, being a part-time mum and blowing all my savings. I guess all of the years of premature maturity had caught up with me, causing me to let off steam, albeit recklessly.

In December 2007, just eight weeks after leaving my long-term relationship, I met another man. He was a great help throughout my struggles, and as quickly as I became reckless, I became grounded once again. I wasn't looking for a relationship at all. I met him through an ad on Facebook for a friendship group called, *Make New Friends*, something which I needed, as all my friends were mutual friends with my ex-partner, and I needed to break free and start afresh.

At the time, his profile picture was of two men and one woman, and I had no idea which man he was. I couldn't view his Facebook profile and didn't know his surname or where he lived. I introduced myself and asked whether he would like to be friends. We exchanged details and added each other to our Facebook profiles, and that's when I realised he lived in Australia. We hit it off right away, as we had many common interests, and it was nice to have a pen pal on the other side of the world.

Over the next few months, we spoke almost daily, and one particular day, he dropped the bombshell that he had feelings for me. He offered to fly me to Australia to meet him, which I declined numerous times. I wasn't ready for a relationship, and as much as I cared for him, I didn't feel the same.

Ten months after meeting him on Facebook and talking daily for the last eight months of that, on webcam, via phone calls and text messages, I gave in to the offer of a holiday, and we finally met in person on 11th November 2008. My father was worried but gave me some spending money and told me to have a good time. He too, had spoken to him on the phone and met him on webcam, but of course, he was worried for me nonetheless. He and I were called all sorts of names by people, such as crazy, stupid, weird, and I found that difficult, but he just didn't have a care in the world about what anyone else thought.

We had an amazing two weeks together. He treated me like his Princess, and we crammed in as many activities and things to do as possible. He made my time the most memorable and magical ever, something which I had never had before and wasn't used to. I was still unsure whether I had feelings for him, whether a relationship could work, or even how it would work, but once I arrived back in England, I knew I wanted to give it a go.

I flew back to Australia two weeks later, just in time for Christmas. I got my first job in years and felt independent, loved and wanted; I could feel myself falling for him. Two months later, on 21st February 2009, we got married, and on the very same day, we announced our pregnancy news. That March, due to being pregnant, I decided to fly back to England to receive maternity care I was familiar with for me and our son. My husband joined me a few months later once his visa had been granted. We spent eight years raising our family in England and went on to have another child, a daughter, in 2013, making our family of five complete. In 2017, we moved back to Melbourne, where we have been ever since.

Life could have been very different for me. I could have used my difficult childhood as an excuse not to be a nice person, but I chose love. I do not hate my mother one little bit; I love her and thank her because as difficult as life was growing up, I couldn't have had a better person than my father to share it with. Everything happens for a reason, and we are all put on this earth for a purpose. We have to be open-minded and willing to learn and understand, not just our own life, but others too, whilst being a little less judgmental along the way, and that's what I do.

I am a mental health practitioner, currently doing extra study on drug and alcohol misuse to further my career, and I am a proud mental health first aider. I advocate for those who have lost their voice. I help and guide those at a loss in life, and I give my clients the tools they need to change their lives. The best reward for me is watching them grow. I live my life as if I was living it for someone else, not literally, but subconsciously, and question whether my decisions would have an unwarranted impact on those around me.

Life is truly what you make of it, and I intend to make sure mine is a happy and memorable one.

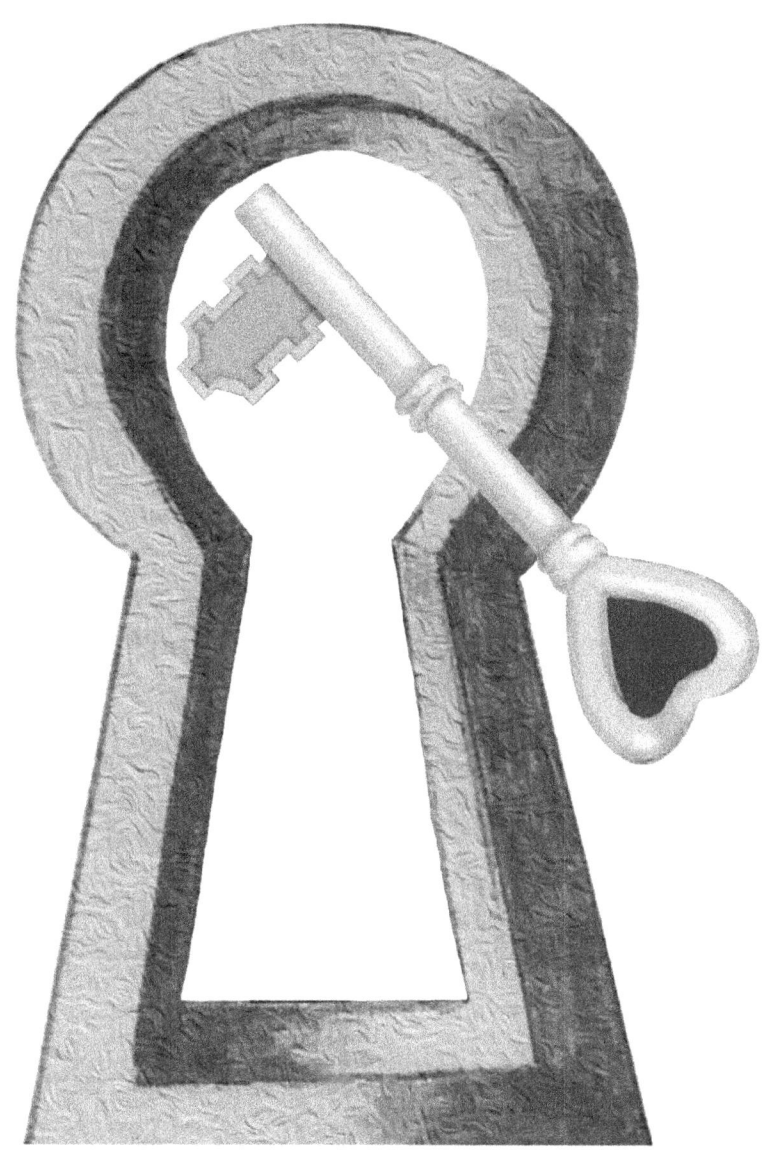

Author Bio

Lisa Locks

Lisa Locks is a mother of two beautiful adult children and their partners, Nanna to two gorgeous grandchildren, and a mum to her dog, Lock-key. Lisa also shares her house with many international students of different nationalities and borders and runs her own hairdressing business from home. There is never a dull moment in her house since there are a lot of people coming in and out every day.

Lisa has always been in tune with her children and others. The realisation of how much love she has for children has inspired her to write a children's book, *What's The Key To My Heart?* (2020)

Lisa understands that every child is different and therefore believes that it is important to provide good, fundamental guidelines, and for each child to know that loving themselves is the key. Once they know that, everything else falls into place.

Lisa's passion for helping children is evident through her fundraising activities, in particular, her support and donations to the River Jordan Orphanage in Kenya, Africa, the Leukemia Foundation and through her participation in the Greatest Shave campaign.

Through the years of hardship of being divorced, raising her two children, and dealing with the constant juggling act of work, school-runs and sports activities that have kept her busy, Lisa has been able to grow as a person and gradually come to understand how to love herself with all her flaws.

She has learned to love and accept herself and has become aware of and taken responsibility for her own decisions. Lisa's positive attitude and her own belief system, which she calls her 'key', underpins her ongoing motivation and commitment and allows her to reach for her dreams and goals.

Perhaps it is Lisa's attitude to life that has enabled others to open up and share their own experiences with her while they are having their hair done. Over the years, Lisa has discovered that her chair becomes therapeutic as people feel comfortable to share their secrets and their stories. This became her inspiration for *Secrets in The Chair*. Lisa thanks all the authors who found the courage to share their secrets and hopes that their stories help and inspire everyone who reads them.

Lisa's determination, even her little feistiness and frustrations, keeps her passion alive which allows her to love and enjoy every minute that she lives.

Lisa aims to 'Live in my thoughts, my feelings and my behaviour - my words are my world.' With this powerful message, Lisa aspires to spread positive energy wherever she goes, thereby shaping future generations.

Her motto is: *Being kind is always on my mind.*

Facebook: https://www.facebook.com/lisa.frood

Instagram: https://www.instagram.com/lisaslocks?igsh=M2IwMGRnN3h0enlj

Email: iamlisalocks@gmail.com

The chair in Lisa Locks' Hairdressing Salon

More From Lisa Locks

What Is The Key To My Heart?

Lisa Locks

Written for children with the aim to inspire and motivate them with a toolbox of positive language that promotes healthy self-talk.

What is the Key to My Heart? is designed to inspire children of all ages and may encourage them to build their confidence one day at a time, and to accept and love themselves and others.

In this book, Lisa Locks helps children understand the importance of routine and structure and how this can help them to discover the tools to live a more fulfilling life. Through the childlike expressions in the book, the reader can identify and start to collect their own tools to better develop their self-esteem.

The book has made it to third-world countries, making many children happy.

Facebook: https://www.facebook.com/lisa.frood

Instagram: https://www.instagram.com/lisaslocks?igsh=M2IwMGRnN3h0enlj

Email: iamlisalocks@gmail.com

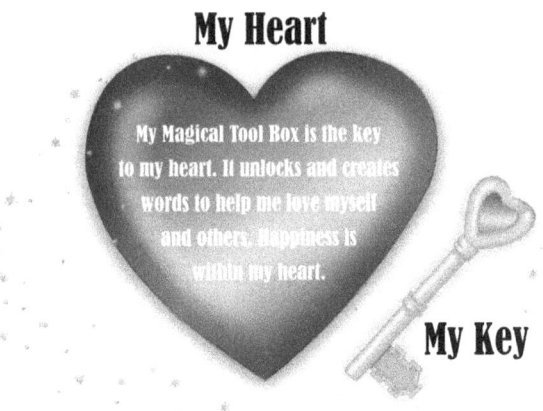

My words in my Magical Tool Box

The Happy Haven Shop

Lisa Lock's Happy Haven Store aims to provide a variety of essentials for living a positive lifestyle for all ages. Our children are our future and require skills and positive reinforcements to help equip them to succeed in their lives.

From mindful activities, gadgets, books and more, this store has it all to help you reset your mind.

iamlisalocks@gmail.com

www.ingramcontent.com/pod-product-compliance
Lightning Source LLC
Chambersburg PA
CBHW062037290426
44109CB00026B/2654